the sacred art of
CHANT

OTHER BOOKS IN THE
PREPARING TO PRACTICE SERIES

The Sacred Art of Bowing:
Preparing to Practice
by Andi Young

The Sacred Art of Fasting:
Preparing to Practice
by Rev. Tom Ryan

the sacred art of
CHANT

preparing
to practice

Ana Hernández

Walking Together, Finding the Way
SKYLIGHT PATHS® Publishing
Woodstock, Vermont

The Sacred Art of Chant:
Preparing to Practice
2005 First Printing
© 2005 by Ana Hernández

For information regarding permission to reprint material from this book, please write or fax your request to SkyLight Paths Publishing, Permissions Department, at the address / fax number listed below, or e-mail your request to permissions@skylightpaths.com.

Library of Congress Cataloging-in-Publication Data
Hernández, Ana.
The sacred art of chant / by Ana Hernández.
    p. cm.—(Preparing to practice)
Includes bibliographical references (p.   ) and index.
ISBN 1-59473-036-9 (pbk.)
    1. Music—Religious aspects. 2. Sacred vocal music—Instruction and study. 3. Spiritual life. I. Title. II. Series.
ML2900.H48 2005
782.2'92143—dc22

2004018554

10 9 8 7 6 5 4 3 2 1
Manufactured in the United States of America
Cover Design and Illustration: Sara Dismukes

SkyLight Paths Publishing is creating a place where people of dif-ferent spiritual traditions come together for challenge and inspira-tion, a place where we can help each other understand the mystery that lies at the heart of our existence.

SkyLight Paths sees both believers and seekers as a community that increasingly transcends traditional boundaries of religion and denomination—people wanting to learn from each other, *walking together, finding the way.*

SkyLight Paths, "Walking Together, Finding the Way" and colophon are trademarks of LongHill Partners, Inc., registered in the U.S. Patent and Trademark Office.

Walking Together, Finding the Way
Published by SkyLight Paths Publishing
A Division of LongHill Partners, Inc.
Sunset Farm Offices, Route 4, P.O. Box 237
Woodstock, VT 05091
Tel: (802) 457-4000   Fax: (802) 457-4004
www.skylightpaths.com

For Ana Maria, Felipe, and Julia

C O N T E N T S

INTRODUCTION

Come down, O love divine, seek Thou this soul of mine,
And visit it with Thine own ardor glowing.
O Comforter, draw near, within my heart appear,
And kindle it, Thy holy flame bestowing.

O let it freely burn, till earthly passions turn
To dust and ashes in its heat consuming;
And let Thy glorious light shine ever on my sight,
And clothe me round, the while my path illuming.

And so the yearning strong, with which the soul will long,
Shall far outpass the power of human telling;
For none can guess its grace, till he become the place
Wherein the Holy Spirit makes His dwelling.

—Bianco da Siena, "Come Down, O Love Divine"

The book you are about to read contains information about
chanting as a spiritual practice. Chanting is exactly the same as
all the other spiritual practices, but it suits me best because it
involves music. Nothing in the world can take me deeper. When
I chant, my entire body is engaged; vibrations permeate me to
the core and can move and transform my energy from one end
of the spectrum to the other and back again. Chanting engages

me totally. Martin Luther had this to say about music and it is equally true about chant: "Nothing on earth is more mighty to make the sad happy and the happy sad, to hearten the downcast, mellow the overweening, temper the exuberant, or mollify the vengeful. The Holy Spirit itself pays tribute to music when it records that the evil spirit of Saul was exorcised as David played upon his harp." Saul must've been a big job.

At some point, I realized the only way I could bring myself to really pray was to sing. The God of organized religion seemed pre-occupied with too many small things, and the people I ran across seemed to think it was more important to explain God endlessly to other people in order to change them (or to make them feel bad if they were unwilling to be changed) than it was to practice unconditional love (which I think is more than enough to deal with for one lifetime). My idea of God is much more incorrigibly loving, patient, and kind, with less "attitude." That's what I need from a God, and if I had it, I would surely share it around. There's a piece of paper in my datebook with a few quotes I've carried for years. They all say essentially the same thing: "God's being immanent depends on us." Abraham Joshua Heschel said that. Teresa of Ávila spells it out in depth: "Christ has no body now on earth but yours; no hands but yours; no feet but yours. Yours are the eyes with which he is to look with compassion on the world; yours the feet on which he is to go about doing good; and yours are the hands with which he is to bless us now." And Lawrence Kushner gets right to the point: "Without our eyes, the Holy One of Being would be blind."

When you carry a thing like that around with you all the time, the impression it makes on you tends to grow the longer you live with it. You clean out your wallet or datebook and find it again, so you read it, and it has the same effect on you all over again, only deeper, because you've thought about it before, and it still feels right. Then you put it away until the next time.

I wondered how I could be God's eyes, hands, and feet. That seemed like biting off more than I could chew. I wondered what gifts I conceivably had that could help with such an undertaking. When I began to approach chant as a spiritual practice, it was a direct result of all this wondering, and because I found that some chants just kept hanging around my brain after I thought I had finished singing. I wondered if they worked the same way as the quotes in my datebook. This intrigued me, because I wanted to know how it was that these tunes kept on keeping on when I wasn't driving them, and because chants are beautiful and fun. But beautiful and fun aren't usually the first words I think about when I think *spiritual discipline*. I wondered about a few other things, but I kept coming back to music.

For years I've kept notebooks with beautiful poems, quotes, and prayers, but would only read through them every now and again when I'd find another good one to add to the book. I began to keep lists of chants as I came across them and to write out the ones I'd never heard before, so I could find them again. I noticed that, as I wrote down a tune, I would have to sing it repeatedly in my head to make sure it was right and that it made me feel good. Soon after, I began to keep an eye out for more chants, and I would find them, or they would be given to me. I still didn't know how this would all play out in my life, but I'm only given some God information on a need-to-know basis.

This is what I've needed to know so far: You can chant anywhere; you can chant in a group, or by yourself. Actually, you can't chant by yourself, because God keeps showing up. It seems God has a big "need to know." That is the point of a spiritual practice, though, isn't it? Finding a way in your life that will repeatedly bring you into a conscious relationship with God. Chanting helps bring to light the kind of God energy that we want to manifest in our lives. It helps us direct ourselves toward the God in us. We may have to dust it off and get reacquainted, but chanting will put us on the right road. After that, all you need to say is "Baby, you can drive my car," and you're on your way. Well, maybe you'll actually have to get in the car every day and help navigate. Chanting is also flexible and helpful. It will remind you which way to go when you don't know, and it doesn't mind spending time lost on a pretty road.

Like other spiritual disciplines, chanting helps us see how we're made in the image of God. Then we begin to notice that everyone else is, too. I don't usually even think of God as a person, but I sometimes I find myself telling people about God in my life based on what I see in the mirror (it seems easier to speak of God in familiar terms when trying to approach matters of the heart). So when I'm writing about my personal experience of God throughout the book, I've chosen to refer to her as a woman. Feel free to change the pronouns if your mirror looks different. Just remember that you are made in that image.

Chanting with an intention to open our hearts and minds to the presence of God in us helps us to be quiet in the face of mystery and learn how to hear what it has to say to us. Chanting can help us focus when we'd normally space out, stay calm when we'd normally blow up, raise our energy level when it's time to go out, lower our energy level when it's time to go to bed (or vice versa—you make the call). Chanting is great at helping us fathom how to deal with our emotions so we don't feel overwhelmed and so we don't overwhelm others: It helps find and maintain a balanced perspective. Or no perspective at all (emptiness is good, too, and often a side benefit). Chanting helps us to be here now (figuratively speaking—I know you're here now). Chanting is healing, fun, and often profound. It can help you to develop your powers of intuition and respect what they have to tell you. Chanting is excellent for transforming your relationships (especially with yourself). Leo Tolstoy once wrote, "Everybody thinks of changing humanity and nobody thinks of changing himself." Chanting is an excellent way to change yourself. On any given day you may be drawn to one chant or another by external circumstances, as well as by internal circumstances. For instance, when I'm feeling impatient, I might use a chant to manifest compassion, both for the external trigger and my internal trigger. Chant is a healthy developmental aid. Chanting provides residual effects, so that even after you've finished, you will still benefit from its presence in your body, like exercise. Chanting is holistic. It will transform you, you will embody the change, and people will notice the new, more grounded you. More important, though, *you* will notice the new, more grounded you.

We spend the first part of our lives becoming who we think we want to be, and in the second part we are supposed to be content with just being. Somewhere in between is the time we begin to reflect on whether or not we're actually who we want to be. We come to a place where our ego consciousness and our soul consciousness play off each other. This is an ongoing process of balancing because issues come and go. Change is constant. Chant helps us work through these changes, so we can have loving, happy, well-integrated lives. Making time for chanting is an investment in our continual becoming.

If you like yourself the way you are, and if your prayer life makes you happy, then go with God and may your life be filled with blessings and peace. On the other hand, if you know you need a little work, have been trying to ignore the fact because some days it looks like it might be a lot of work, and your prayer life is starting to look less like spiritual evolution and more like a laundry list of "shoulds," then this is your lucky day.

Welcome to the world of chant.

You may have noticed the apple on the cover. Okay, maybe not, but it's still there. God's that way too. If you cut an apple crosswise, you get a view of the core. Luckily, God's figured out a way for us to view our core without being cut crosswise. The core of an apple has what looks like the petals of a flower with seeds surrounded by a lot of white. In us, the white part is light, and the seeds will do what seeds do: grow us. The apple is associated with the heart chakra (we explore chakras in chapter 3) and is a symbol of wholeness and maturity.

The heart is at the center of our life's expedition, and it is all about love. As you might suspect, love is intimate. Love attracts more love. A Hasidic sage once said, "The relationship between God and the human soul was never intended to be platonic." If you've ever had a feeling that God is closer than the foundation of the nearest sacred site, you're right: God's right here, holding this book. Don't doubt it for a minute.

In my relationship with God, I aim for many things—fun, insight, the ability to attend to detail yet not be obsessed with the small stuff, and so on. I've noticed that achieving these aims requires me to love my inner self in a deeper, more intimate way. It's both a challenge and a blessing.

Right about now you're probably wondering, "What kind of spiritual practice is this fabled chant?" So, maybe not "fabled chant," but I think that first part's right. As a spiritual practice, chant is what you and God make of it. I'm just here to give you some tools that point to the light at your core.

Inside this book you'll find chants to various aspects of God, even the Goddess of abundance and the God of destruction. However, it's not as if a pile of cash will show up at your door or you'll have ultimate power if you use them. You might, however, find yourself with a more abundant attitude and uncharacteristically open to ideas and options that had previously gone unrecognized. Or, you might be able to find closure within yourself for an externally unresolved event. This book won't get you everything you want in life, but it might help you to want what's given to you, figure out what you really need (and don't need), and help you to discern the part of that you already possess. The best part of the whole venture is that God will be right there, in every breath you take.

CHAPTER ONE

WHY I CHANT AND HOW I STARTED (A PRETTY ROAD INTO A THICKET)

I often think of my mind as a thicket, filled with so many things piled one on top of the other, all tangled up, stuffed full of a lifetime of living, with the occasional thornbush lying in wait, ready to draw blood. It's a very crowded and noisy place, much like this sentence. I've always been fascinated with ideas about God, love, beauty, a clean planet, laughter, justice for everyone, and a peaceful world (in no particular order). I don't know when or how, or who put the idea into my head, but somewhere along the way I realized at a deep level that the external peace that I wished for the world could only happen if it was possible to find internal peace. "Just great," I thought. "What a job! Time to clear out the thicket. Where's the machete? It's a jungle in here!" You will not believe the load of junk I found. People I used to know, bad dreams, things done and left undone, things I ought not to have done, things done to me that ought not to have been done. Suffice it to say that it will probably take the rest of my life to clean up the mess (I'm considering applying for Superfund status). At first, I thought I was unique. But then I began to notice that everyone else has much the same thicket to deal with. I found it oddly comforting, knowing that I'm not the only one. (Lesson No. 1: All people are more fragile than you might imagine, and maybe just as fragile as you.)

You may be thinking, "What does this have to do with chant?" For me, chant has everything to do with life. I have such a huge cleanup task ahead of me that the only way I can lead a happy life is to take a beautiful road directly into the middle of my thicket. That way, no matter what happens, or whomever I meet, I am still on the prettiest road. And the way I'm able to walk happily on the road through the thicket is by chanting.

Why chant? Chant is the one spiritual discipline I've found that helps me with all of the rest of life. It even helps me enjoy other spiritual disciplines (go figure). Chanting helps me to listen for the here and now, giving me a better grip on reality; it improves my receptivity and focus; it helps me to remain open when I'd rather say, "Thanks, but no thanks"; it helps me connect with my inner world; it prevents me from feeling overwhelmed by life (so far). Chant grounds and calms me, and if I'm tired, I can use it to raise my energy level; it opens me to things I find uncomfortable and painful in such a way that I'm able to work through the pain and discomfort. Chanting helps me to be a better listener by helping me remain emotionally and spiritually available to whomever God sends through the door, enabling me to hear and see what people are actually saying beyond the words they use. It allows my intuition to be more accessible in my everyday life, which means I have more to work with than the mere reliance on that roiling, amorphous gut feeling that tells me "something's up." Chanting can be a raft in a storm, even a luxury liner sometimes—not often, but occasionally. I'm sure it's helped to keep me off the streets and out of the loony bin (although I like the tunes in there). Sometimes chanting is hard work, but other times it flows like water.

I don't really know how I started to chant. What initially prompted my brain to latch on to music the way it does is a mystery to me. It's not as if I woke up one day and realized, "Hey, I'm wired for sound!" Or did I? No matter; the sounds of life in general just thrill me. I love sound. I love making sounds. I think that making sound is just about as much fun as a girl can have with her clothes on, and clothes are not a requirement. It doesn't get much better than that. I'm a simple person at heart, sometimes in a way other people can't understand.

I am happy to simply sing harmony along with the hum of the refrigerator, most other appliances, and the commuter train. I spend way too much time turning any poor little resonant object that crosses my path into a musical instrument to sing with. Sound helps me feel. There's nothing like the feeling when making a good, long, low, ahhhhh sound. Sound cheers me up when nothing else can penetrate a foul mood. Sound brings me back to myself in a way that mere thoughts cannot. The return to my body is so fast it's like being beamed back home.

I am clearly possessed by music. My mother told me that in my crib I would make a particular sound when a certain song played on the radio. This song, it seems, had a sound in the middle that wasn't like all the other sounds, and I picked it out as a jewel to be honored (or something like that). I am, of course, too embarrassed to actually figure out which song or sound it could have been that thrilled me so as an infant, but I've seen it happen fairly often ever since. I've met other sounds in my life that for no apparent reason have forced themselves into my brain and never let go.

I'm sure you also have sounds that stick in your head. There are those of us to whom sounds stick like glue. Remember the *Gilligan's Island* theme song? Television jingles? Your favorite song on the radio, from the summer after sixth grade ("Sooner or later, love is gonna get ya …")? Your mother's favorite song, a theme from a symphony, or any little tune that seems to set itself spinning in your brain? I know you know. They emerge from the dark recesses of our minds (where they're supposed to be safely buried) to torture us with their endless loops once again. I call them viruses. Initially, these little viral tunes come unbidden, which is preferable, because why would anyone deliberately summon the *Magilla Gorilla* theme song? Sometimes I wake up in the morning and there they are, and there I lie, unarmed, with no way to stop them. I've heard tell of a mystical product called TuneBGone, but until I can find it in the grocery store, round and round they go. I have asked God to please make it stop, but it seems God's got bigger fish to fry.

I also remember, though, learning about the beauty and staying power of a *cantus firmus* (fixed melody) used as the foundation or ground for the weaving and spinning of counterpoint around it. It all started with the Beatles' "All You Need Is Love," followed closely by Monteverdi's *Magnificat* ("Song of Mary"). We sang the Monteverdi in high school, and I would wake up in the morning with it already turned on in my head, or I would be sitting in a class and poof! "There it is again!" over and over and over. This was entirely different from a virus; this kind of tune made me feel good, actually gave me more energy, and didn't just distract me. This seemed worthy of further investigation.

Being myself and not some organized person, I promptly forgot about that kind of mystical tune for about twenty years. Oh, I still sang lots of classical and sacred music in choirs and folk music in coffeehouses, but there was something missing. My heart just wasn't into the commercial part of it. Most of the music didn't move me, and the entertainment songs you had to sing to "make it" in those places seemed to breed particular types of people who thought in particular ways. I don't know how I think— I just occasionally find myself thinking. It's still a surprise, this reflective bone I've got, but I believe it keeps me feeling more comfortable living on the margins rather than in the middle of a group of people. Don't get me wrong, I really like people—I just want *all* of the people to be able to play at my party. If a place starts to feel like a members-only club to me, I am outta there.

For many years I sang in choirs. I've sung in volunteer choirs, professional choirs, and choirs that were a combination of both, singing all kinds of music. Basically, the more professional the choir, the less I was able to locate God in the experience. Although the quality of the music was high, it was not enough for me to be a part of making beautiful music while there were ugly relationships going on underneath. I watched choir directors turn red in the face while they yelled at people during rehearsals for singing the wrong notes, or for singing them the wrong way. I was usually the choir's alto section leader, and wiseass. But even I would go home tied up in knots, after I would try to help the people learn their parts so they wouldn't be yelled at again. There wasn't a lot of joy in these experiences. For a while I thought it was okay to bring spiritual sustenance to others but not worry about my own spiritual sustenance. If I made other people happy, then that was enough. Besides, I was making twenty-five bucks an hour to sing! But, ultimately, it isn't enough to take care of others or to make other people happy if you don't take care of yourself. I figured this out because I was sitting with Jon, my spiritual director, and he said something along the lines of "So, when are you going to start taking care of what you need to make *you* happy?" I hate it when people turn on you like that, don't you? Here I was, trying to do what I thought I was supposed to be doing for other folks, and this snippy monk comes along and turns the question around.

Well, what *did* I need to make me happy? It turned out that the answer was the beginning of a different way of relating to most of what I thought I knew. I already had someone who loved me and surprised me daily, not to mention having the best dog on the planet, so all I really needed was a simple song that anyone could sing. A tune simple enough to learn in a minute, but one that would stick with me in a positive way. I figured that since

I'm wired for sound—God having installed a top-of-the-line sound card on my hard drive—it might actually be a gift, and I might as well try to make good use of it. So, I decided that my hard drive needed some great software. Simple tunes are my software.

WE ALL NEED A SIMPLE TUNE

I spend a lot of my time on the quest for a simple tune, hummed while washing the dishes or driving the car. A simple tune, humming me to the place that has been calling as long as I can remember. A simple tune, breathing me in and out, over and over, renewing my strength, bolstering my resolve. A simple tune, simple enough to be sung by everyone—simple enough so we can all forget for the moment about how we came to be humming this tune at this time. A simple tune that seems to be humming us toward the places we're feeling called to. A simple tune, one that you can just sing because it gets you there, wherever you intend your "there" to be. Enough simple tunes for everyone, drawers filled with simple tunes showing up like mismatched socks—for the long line at the grocery store, for the waiting room at the hospital, for all of us at work, for getting the flu shot, for giving the flu shot, for rowing a boat, for the picket lines, for the library (a very soft, simple tune), and for taking out the garbage (accompanied by trash can lids). Tunes for unexpected guests arriving at inappropriate times (I think the beginning of that one is "Where have all the towels gone?"). Tunes to usher us in and out of all the transitions, big and small: tunes for the births and deaths, the long healings (maybe a nice, slow, green tune), the not-healings, the uncertainties, and the not-having-a-clue-what-to-do-next times. A tune to give us the guts to speak the truth to power, another to help us hold our tongue when we are about to blow it by speaking that last terrible thing, and one to help us stop and make ourselves rest before we run out of emotional, physical, and spiritual gas.

A simple tune that calls forth the vibrations around us and brings me out of myself to experience them with you. A simple tune to help me pray and to help me to help you pray and another for when we're apart (and maybe one or two that you only share with God). A simple tune to help me hear through your pain and anger to what you are trying to say, and another to help you hear through my pain and anger (maybe that's the same tune, or maybe we just sing it backwards and meet in the middle). One to assuage guilt and shame. A simple tune to help us manifest our sweetest selves. Another one to help us settle down and listen to the wind in the trees, one to sing along to the rhythm of the waves, one in thanksgiving for the beauty of the rivers, one for the lakes, and one to hum with the owls (or the dog, or the cat) as we drift off to sleep.

A simple tune to help us all reach the place where the world is breathing, has been breathing since before breath and spirit were the same thing. A simple tune to renew our spirits, tune us up, find our balance, and keep us attuned. A simple tune to make you laugh. A simple tune to calm the babies before they sleep (there are a lot of these around already—may desperation drive us to song in other situations as well). A simple tune for the bad dreams, to ameliorate them and restore us to our sweet selves (this one might be a four-part chant, but "rain, rain go away" comes to mind).

Sure, simple tunes can be hard to come by in this world that seems so often out of tune. But a wise man once said, "Sometimes heaven is just a new pair of glasses."

SOUND, THE CAUSE OF EVERYTHING

What if we were to actively engage music in an effort to grow spiritually? What if we were to collect chants based on their topical efficacy? To consciously use music to affect our subconscious minds in a way that would help us to transcend our minds and work on our hearts? How would we change, if at all? Is it possible to use sound to help us to feel more comfortable inside our own skin? To transcend the limits we impose on ourselves? To open the gates to the parts of us that we don't want to look at and befriend them? To remove the obstacles we continually place in the middle of our own paths?

Here we both are, sitting, quietly reading these words, and our bodies are pumping, buzzing, swishing, and ticking fairly loudly. And doing these things without getting in the way of our reading this. At its most basic level, sound is merely vibration. Nothing big, only the cause of everything.

What if the path life is supposed to take is actually meant to be connected to your heart? Not just the things that move you, although that's as good a place to start as any, but the things that transform you. It's not as far-fetched as you might think. Even the Grinch had his heart grow two sizes the day he finally got off his ass and drove his sled down the mountain to sing with the villagers. Now his intention wasn't the most pure when he set out, to say the least, but there's no telling what happens once you start off down any given hill and find a tune waiting for you at the bottom. There is absolutely no reason on God's green earth to think that I, a Puerto Rican, trumpet-playing lesbian from Long Island, should find her heart's desire in the care and feeding of a chant practice and in teaching chants to others. (Lesson No. 2: God is incredibly huge and very quirky, of this I am sure.)

When music possesses me it frees me to be a companion to myself, and somehow leads me into companionship with others. Paradoxically, music is also the vehicle I use to transcend time. The vehicle I've found that consistently gets me to the place beyond time the fastest is chant—almost all kinds of chant. I have a regular chant practice, by which I mean five days a week, between thirty and seventy-five minutes a day, depending on the rhythms of my life. I use mantra, plainsong, Native American chants, chants in Sanskrit, Hebrew, Latin, English, Zuni, and Spanish, mainly, with new chants coming and going. I tend toward a more informal practice, because I have a fairly busy life. God has blessed me with two vocations, for which blessing I have been known to curse back. By day, I sell books about God; by night, I am a musician.

Actually, I'm a musician all the time, but God gave me other gifts to help keep me off the street, for which blessing I am exceedingly thankful (cursing and thanking are two of the main ways God and I communicate). Anyway, these gifts help me to make money, and they are like coins in another sense, too: They have a flip side. We say, "Heads or tails," when we flip a coin for who goes first in a game—and through chanting I've found that I have to pay attention to the downside in life as well. When we flip in a game, the person who loses the toss still plays in the game, but before I began chanting in earnest, I chose not to look at the painful parts of my life, the annoying parts, the confusing parts, and so on, because they were too much work to deal with. Then one day, after having a fight with the person I love most in the universe, I was chanting, and I started to do some serious reflection about what had happened to make a seemingly innocuous encounter blow up in my face. I noticed that I'd done things that weren't particularly smart, and I vowed to try to pay attention to what part I'd played in getting us to such a terrible place. The hardest part was that the fight had happened just when everything seemed to be going better than ever. So, what to do? I'd just gone from experiencing this relationship as the best of all possible worlds to wondering if I belonged in a relationship at all! How was I to make sense of that?

As I was chanting, it dawned on me that one of the best things God ever gave me was the gift of reflection. It's a good gift for me, because I don't always get things right the first time, or even the first twenty. I think most of the time we're barely aware of the most important tools we've been given. Until this particular fight, I had hardly realized that reflection was a gift. It was just something I did constantly, like breathing or humming or singing. Now, however, I finally understood that I could use sound and reflection to work through the things I didn't like to look at, and the old stories I tell myself while on autopilot. They may have served me well until now, and gotten me this far, but are they still necessary? I remember reading something Parker Palmer said about how our limits are the flip side of our gifts. In his book *Let Your Life Speak,* he writes, "A particular weakness is the inevitable trade-off for a particular strength. We will become better teachers not by trying to fill the potholes in our souls but by knowing them so well that we can avoid falling into them."

I've got a few inner potholes that show up fairly regularly, and it's all I can do to not try to fix them. I'm pretty good at avoiding the actual potholes in the road each winter, but when life gets rough and discouraging, I tend to fall right into the interior ones. That's when chanting can help you save your life, and help to avoid those costly repairs to your undercarriage.

THE CONSCIOUS EAR

Dr. Alfred Tomatis (1920–2001) was a French ear, nose, and throat physician, a psychologist, and a surgeon. He demonstrated that the ear and the voice are inextricably bound together by their functions. His research with opera singers showed that the voice can only produce what it can hear. This may seem to be a pretty simple observation, but in practical terms it means that listening matters more than we think it does. There are currently more than two hundred Tomatis centers in the world, and the doctor's fifty years of work is being used to help people with autism, attention deficit and hyperactivity disorders, dyslexia, Asperger's syndrome, Down's syndrome, learning delays, and balance and coordination problems. He also showed that one of the main functions of the ear is to charge the brain with energy. How does it do that? By the way it processes sounds. Dr. Tomatis is the reason many more women today speak to their children while they're still in the womb. The ear is one of the first organs to develop, and Tomatis was the first person to demonstrate that there is a dialogue that happens well before we are born. He also believed that hearing connects us to the Divine.

He was once called to a Benedictine monastery in France for a consultation. It was a community of ninety brothers, and the new abbot, a young man, had decided to make the rule of the order more modern. Benedictines usually spend hours a day chanting in prayer, because:

> As the prophet says: "Seven times in the day so I praise Thee." Which sacred number of seven will thus be fulfilled by us if, at matins, at the first, third, sixth, ninth hours, at vesper time and at completorium [Compline, the last office of the day, traditionally said before going to bed] we perform the duties of our service; for it is of these hours of the day that he said: "Seven times in the day do I praise Thee." For, concerning nocturnal vigils, the same prophet says: "At midnight I arose to confess unto thee." Therefore, at these times, let us give thanks to our Creator concerning the judgments of his righteousness; that is, at matins, etc.... and at night we will rise and confess to him.
>
> —Benedictine Rule, chapter 16

"Seven times in the day so I praise Thee." I figure the monks chanted about fifteen or twenty minutes at each of the offices, one of which is done in the middle of the night. The schedules of monks have always been a model for industriousness, but these guys probably only slept four to five hours a night. Since chanting the daily offices takes longer than speaking them, the abbot convinced the monks that the time spent chanting could be better spent on other things, and so they stopped chanting. As time went on, they began to get sluggish, and became more and more tired. They had a meeting and decided that they needed to get more sleep, like other people. So they started going to bed early. Physiologically, though, the more you sleep, the more tired you get, so they continued on their downward spiral. Then the abbot brought in a nutritionist, who decided that they must be suffering from starvation, because they were mostly vegetarians. He prescribed meat and potatoes, which made things even worse. Finally, they called Dr. Tomatis, who over the course of a couple of months figured out that the monks had been using chant to charge their systems. Without the chant seven times a day, there were a number of signs that their energy was sagging, not least of which was the fact that he found most of the monks "slumping in their cells."

Dr. Tomatis used only sound to retrain their ears, and in a few months' time they were all back at their tasks, and singing their offices seven times a day (may I mention at ungodly hours?), eating their vegetarian diet, and serving their community.

There are a couple of important things to be learned from this story that are directly applicable to our spiritual lives. The Benedictine monks chanted Gregorian chant. One of the main effects this type of chant has on our bodies is its ability to draw us up out of our bodies. What this means, spiritually speaking, is that chant provides a huge charge to our cerebral cortex, which is the part of our brain that we use to get us to that higher place of prayer. A lot of energy is required for us to be able to get beyond what the Buddhists call our "monkey mind," the place where, as soon as we sit down to pray, a laundry list of thoughts starts flying through, distracting us with things like bills, meetings, appointments, and even doing the laundry (insert your own list here).

One of the functions of the ear is to translate the sound vibrations that we receive through our skin and bones and all the things that send sound into us. When the monks stopped chanting, not only did they lose the benefit of sound vibrating in their bodies, but they lost the benefits derived from sound vibrating on their bodies that came from the voices of their brothers, as well as the charge it provided, which they needed to get them to the level at which they were used to experiencing prayer. They also lost the residual charge, that part of the chanting that stayed with them, maintaining their energy level in a way that enabled them to keep such a schedule. The more frustrated they became, the more energy they expended to try to overcome it, and the more tired they got.

I hope to be able, throughout the course of this book, to share with you the ways I've found to use the gift of the voice God gave you to develop and look after your spiritual life, using chant. Join me on a pretty road into your own thicket, and remember: God never leads you into a pothole that's too deep to get out of.

> Thirty spokes will converge in the hub of a wheel; but the use of the cart will depend on the part of the hub that is void.
> With a wall all around a clay bowl is molded; but the use of the bowl will depend on the part of the bowl that is void.
> Cut out the windows and doors in the house as you build; but the use of the house will depend on the space in the walls that is void.
> So advantage is had from whatever is there; but usefulness rises from whatever is not.
> —Lao Tzu, *Tao Te Ching* (No. 11)

WHO CHANTS, AND WHERE? FINDING YOUR VOICE

The whole of life in all its aspects is one music, and to tune
oneself to the harmony of this perfect music is the real spiritual attainment.

—Hazrat Inayat Khan

Anyone can chant. It doesn't matter if people have told you all
your life that you can't sing. They were wrong. God gave us all
a voice, and it's our job to figure out how to use it. I think it's
probably the hardest task we've got to accomplish. Since I'm not
endowed with incredible superpowers, I've had to do it the old-
fashioned way: by trial and error.

The first thing I figured out was that it's important to me to
have a space to chant that encourages a quietness of spirit or a
sense of clarity—a place that fosters the openness and trans-
parency and vulnerability that help me to reach that God place.
If I'm at home, I tend to chant in my room. At one end, I've

placed a shelf on the top of a radiator, and on it I've placed a statue of Kuan Yin (Buddhist bodhisattva of compassion) and a small keepsake box that contains some items I value. I guess you could call it my altar, although it doesn't have a beautiful cloth, or too much of anything really, that would make someone think it was an altar. The shelf is at one end of the room; there's a window that receives morning sun and a round meditation cushion for sitting on the rug. The only time I use the space is when I chant, so I have no trouble going inside myself, whereas when I chant at the river on my way to work, there are always distractions (big, loud trains, hungry birds, etc.). And when I'm chanting while doing the dishes or the laundry, there's always the dishes or the laundry to deal with. When I sit in my room, even though the rest of the room may be covered in books and instruments, there's only the shelf, the window, the cushion, me, and God. I usually sit for a few minutes in silence before I begin chanting, and I turn off the ringer on the phone, close the door, and light a candle or a stick of incense. I have a routine that I generally stick to, but sometimes chants show up before I know what I'm doing: "Oooh! Pick me!" I sometimes do pick them—it depends on the day, and each day is different. I guess what I'm trying to say is that it's helpful to have a place that I only use for chanting. This way, when I go there, that's all I do. It seems to have its own momentum some days, especially when I'm tired. It creates its own energy. I know writers who simply go into their offices and turn on the computer, light a candle, and begin writing. That's what they're there for, so it makes it harder to be distracted.

But what happens, what security, what joy to have someone to whom you dare to speak on terms of equality as to another self, one to whom you can unblushingly make known what progress you have made in the spiritual life; one to whom

you can entrust all the secrets of your heart and before
whom you can place all your plans.

—Aelred of Rievaulx

When I sit in my room, I trust that God isn't going to give
me a hard time, which makes me feel a little more comfortable
digging deep. I haven't always been able to find my voice, and I
have suffered from stage fright, butterflies, nerves, whatever you
want to call it. Early on, I began to notice that I did just fine
when the people around me were supportive and kind, and it
probably took me until I was in my mid-thirties to realize that
when the people around me were competitive or driven, tense,
controlling, or whatever rotten attitude affected the energy in
the room, I sang badly and wasn't particularly well behaved,
shall we say, because I was less secure in the atmosphere. I can
get an attitude when I feel disrespected. Chanting has helped me
be more consistent in my singing and in daily life by keeping me
mindful of the one atmosphere over which I have the most control—my body/mind/spirit/soul. Take a minute or two and focus
on what has helped to strengthen your voice and what has ham-
pered it. Write your insights down. I call this my getting-to-
know-you exercise.

Chanting has helped me to pay attention so that I am more
discerning of the energy in a room and how it might affect people, by listening to how it's affecting me. I am even a little more
confident in my ability to change the energy in an uncomfortable
room just by singing. When I was younger, I would be thrown
off guard by such energy; I now understand that if I walk into a
room and the energy is out of whack, most likely it has nothing
to do with me. Maybe 95 percent of the time it has nothing to do
with me. The energy can still affect me if I let it in, sure, but I
now have the tools to affect *it* just by making sound in the space
for ten minutes or so. (Feeling more self-assured helps me tend
to my gifts in a way that enables me to focus on what's going on

around me.) Besides, it's always nice to feel that you have a grip on a situation.

Once, at the beginning of a conference on sacred music, as I walked into the big room where we were to spend a large part of the next three days, four people were leaving hurriedly. A fifth person followed me into the room, and as we introduced ourselves, we both sensed something not quite right. We walked around the room (as I always like to walk around in a new place to get the feel of it), and my new friend took out her instruments and began playing around. At some point, we looked at each other and agreed that there was some bad energy hanging around. We found a spot where the air just felt heavy and decided to try to shift the energy a little. Bad energy is not conducive to a good conference. We had no idea what we were dealing with until later in the evening, when it became clear that there were some power and control issues among the organizers, and there had been a disagreement in the space right before we'd arrived. It had taken almost twenty minutes to change the residual energy from the sounds of their disagreement from an icky feeling to one where a little more openness might be facilitated. Do I even have words to describe this adequately? Why is it that sound tends to linger in a place? How is it that both the positive and negative aspects of a particular sound can remain in a space long after the speakers have moved on? I do not have an answer for that, but I've seen the upside also.

I was in a church in Teaneck, New Jersey, last year for a Martin Luther King Jr. Day service. Afterward, there was a gathering in the parish hall, and I led some chanting interspersed with poems read by their authors. There was quite a good atmosphere in that room, filled with more than a hundred people. After about three minutes of simple humming, we spontaneously stopped. The note we were singing did not. The sound lingered in the room for well over a minute. People looked at each other and up at the ceiling, which seemed to be holding on to the sound.

It almost sounded like the rafters were answering us! No one made a peep, it was so beautiful, and people broke out in smiles all around the room. When it finally stopped, there were many audible exhales, and a couple of "Wows!" The rest of the session was divinely inspired because the sound opened us up to another dimension of reality. Sound lingers in our bodies in much the same way. We are affected by whatever is "in the air" in ways we routinely ignore or downplay, but we have the capacity to manage our reactions and choose our responses. Chant is a good way to practice becoming aware of how our particular autopilot operates.

On an emotional level, I understand the power of sound. It can both attract and repel. Because words have been used in the past to hurt me (as with many of us), I have learned the hard way that it's more important to be kind than to be clever. In a situation where I'm in a group, there are always those who are more comfortable making sound and those who are less comfortable. It's really important for me—as an itinerant noise-maker—to try to be mindful of those not like me and to encourage them by listening to them when they speak. I'm not always good at this, but if I can pay attention long enough, it's possible to hear people into speech or song. If I can help someone feel comfortable and safe by mindfully including them, I find that God is great at bringing the rest of the party. So I intentionally sit next to the hard of hearing who are brave enough to attend my workshops, and I speak slowly and clearly for the blind when giving instructions, because I want them to be able to join in with everyone else, and usually the sighted have the benefit of some kind of handout to refer to. The blind depend on the repetition and tend to memorize the chants. I sit across from the people who seem fragile or skittish so I can pay attention and give encouragement, and not intimidate them with my big mouth. Mychal Judge, a Franciscan priest and chaplain with the New York Fire Department, carried around this prayer before he was killed on September 11, 2001:

Lord, Take me where you want me to go;
Let me meet who you want me to meet;
Tell me what you want me to say;
And keep me out of your way.

We could adapt this as practical advice for chanting: Show up, be present, and stay out of the way.

PREPARING THE GROUND

I love gardens and flowers, but I don't always enjoy digging in the dirt. If I think the flowers will be better off in a different place, though, I move them. My inner life is like a garden, not one of those beautifully tended and pruned, symmetrical Italianate types of garden, but more like a riot of flowers, an English cottage garden—everything leaning over every other thing, and climbing all over the house. Gardens are a pretty big metaphor in all the holy books. When I planted the cherry tree in my front yard two years ago, the instructions said that in order to grow a happy and healthy tree, I should dig the hole twice as wide and a little bit deeper than the root ball. I remember thinking that's how I'd like my mind to be: really broad and a little bit deep. The instructions also said that if I had a fifteen-dollar tree, I'd need a thirty-dollar hole. That made me laugh, and then it made me think. Now I imagine each individual chant as a fifteen-dollar tree, and my body as the thirty-dollar hole. It's easy to be self-deprecatory and dismissive when I think about myself as the hole: huge, gaping, and without light. It's a bit more labor intensive and humbling to reflect on myself as the environment that is supposed to accept the seed and nurture it until it becomes a big, strapping tree that birds might like to build their nests in.

I present a lot of workshops where I help people to find their voices, but I'm still trying to find mine. It's a lifetime process, finding your voice. Every day brings a new situation that you may or may not be ready for, physically, emotionally, spiritually: a difficult person, an unfamiliar pain in a new part of your body (the thirty-dollar hole), the pain of a loved one. Many of the people I deal with in workshops are priests, therapists, and other health care professionals, and what never ceases to amaze me is the gap between the way people take care of the others in their lives but can't seem to find the time or energy to take care of themselves. I can't be thankful enough for this one lesson (No. 3): You must prepare your own ground before you can help others prepare their ground. You cannot be a wilting flower and expect to be able to carry a full bucket of water to your friend's garden. It doesn't work (and not just because flowers can't carry buckets, either).

Finding your voice is something like that. Even Shakespeare said, "Self-love is not so vile a sin as self-neglecting." There is a voice inside trying to speak to you. If you listen closely, it will reveal itself to you, day by day. For me, the most difficult part of listening closely is being able to quiet my head for a long enough time so that I can hear my heart speak. If left to my own devices, I have difficulty getting focused, much less staying focused. I've found some friends along the way that I'd like to share with you. They make that task a lot more manageable. Words and music (not necessarily in that order) are the two things that can almost instantaneously take me to another place. In his book *Music and Imagination,* Aaron Copland says, "This never ending flow of music forces us to use our imaginations, for music is in a continual state of becoming." So are we in a continual state of becoming, although it might seem easier to ignore that particular ode to change.

The pianist Glenn Gould put it a little differently: "The purpose of art is not the release of a momentary ejection of adrenaline, but is, rather, the lifelong construction of a state of wonder and serenity." It's okay with me if it takes my whole life to overcome the obstacles, because it's taken my whole life so far to set them up, and more are sure to come along. Nevertheless, building a state of wonder and serenity is nothing to scoff at. Every day, I do a little work on my state, infusing it with love, a lot of laughter and song, and the occasional vase of flowers. I'm more inclined to listen attentively and not just try to figure out what I want to say in response while you're talking (momentary release of adrenaline). Lesson No. 4: You show respect by just listening, and you learn more than you can imagine. It's important to help others to build their own states of wonder and serenity, and to hear about their states. We build a reciprocity, looking more and more like ourselves, both to ourselves and to each other, even if we don't necessarily look wondrously serene 24/7.

Another step on the road to the state of wonder and serenity is knowing yourself. This sometimes seems more like a four-lane road without a crosswalk and can seem like it takes a lifetime, but luckily, time is suspended here: In the state of wonder and serenity you can live many lifetimes at once, making the job a little easier. When Glenn Gould played the piano, he grunted a lot while he was playing. Maybe this kept him focused. I blow air through pursed lips when I'm really concentrating. It was pointed out to me once by my partner, and now I know that I do it. I think of it like blowing on kindling to light a fire, but I try not to let it scare others (frighten the horses, as they say). I wonder if Gould knew he was grunting. He was lucky that the recording equipment of his day wasn't digital, or I'm sure he'd have gotten a lot more grief about it. I have a recording of him playing the Goldberg Variations that is oh so beautiful, but if you listen really carefully, you can hear him grunting. Brings a smile to my heart. For me, knowing thyself doesn't mean being capable of not making the noises, but being aware of the propensity to make them, and paying enough attention to be able to minimize their occurrence in inappropriate venues.

Knowing thyself in chant terms means gaining an understanding of how the sound is made by your body, where it lives in your body, and when to use which sounds for what. Getting a handle on this helps build beautiful rooms in the state of wonder and serenity.

CHANT IN THE REAL WORLD

There are days when I can find my voice and days when I'm so paralyzed with fear and insecurity on a personal level, and confusion, overwork, and a general bad feeling on a corporate level, that I can hardly speak.

Today, for instance, it was the corporate level. Every encounter seemed fraught. I went to get a train after work to go to play a Taizé-type service at the cathedral, and the hallway to the train was roped off. Okay, so I tried to go around by a different way. I finally reached the platform after the fourth detour, and I was turned away by the police. I began to walk to my alternate subway choice, and as I neared the end of the tunnel, there was an announcement that my original train was back in service. Back I walked, another block and a half, and I got on the train. Great, I thought, because all of this schlepping was done lugging thirty pounds of instruments (Lesson No. 5: Chanting is hard work). I arrived at the cathedral thirty minutes before the service and walked back to the chapel, and it was locked. No one in sight. So I sat on the floor and chanted.

Twenty minutes later, someone showed up and had a key. I went in, set up, and tuned. The clergyperson came in, said hi, and then walked out. "Wait, I have a question—" I said. No matter that we'd never spoken before and were going to lead a prayer service together in ten minutes—she had something more important to do. I sat down, began to sound the singing bowl to center myself in the room. She came back in and asked me at what tempo I was going to do a particular song. (This chant has a text by Teresa of Ávila and is called *Nada te Turbe,* which means "Nothing shall trouble." It's beautiful, and one of my favorites, but I have never even thought about what tempo I do it at. I've been doing it for years.) I tried to think if anyone had ever asked me at what tempo I was going to play a tune, and I couldn't come up with a split-second answer. I was wary because I sensed this question was coming from some earlier experience she'd had. So, I asked if she had one in mind, and she looked at me blankly. I felt as if I'd avoided a trap by not just launching into some wrong tempo—whatever that might be. I offered that it would be a comfortable tempo, not too fast, so that English-speaking people could sing the Spanish words without tripping over them. She seemed to think this was a good idea. I asked her about another tune that we'd used the previous week that we hadn't communicated about, and during which she'd made hand signals. I don't like hand signals unless I have some idea of what they mean (I prefer those orange semaphore flags). I thought we had it all squared away, and she went back to her seat.

This short chant service was one of the least prayerful (for me) of my life, because during the next thirty minutes, the woman kept making this hand signal that just confused me. You try: I'm sitting across a circle from you, and you're singing and playing the accompaniment for the congregation. It's the middle of the tune. I point my finger at you. Do I want you to stop playing? Or, do I want you to play one more time? Or, is there a huge monster behind you that you need to look out for? Don't know? Me neither. The one time *I* needed clarification, her eyes were closed in prayer. Now, she was "in charge" of this service, but I'm sure she didn't see herself as having any power. Keep an eye out for this phenomenon: The powers who love to exert control rarely see themselves as powerful, and don't communicate very well (Lesson No. 6).

I sometimes think that my chant practice will enhance my intuition and help me to tune in to what's going on in a situation like that, but that is, as they say, an unrealistic expectation. I'm sometimes very tuned in, and other times I'm thick as a brick. My energy level, how much sleep I've had, what my day has been like, whether or not I've sung, or had coffee—any of these things can contribute to my intuition or lack of it. Some days you're building a state of wonder and serenity, and other days it's all you can do not to interrupt the flow of a service to yell across the room: "What are you trying to tell me?" It's all how you feel, and your feelings often lie.

Lesson No. 7: Communication is one of the most important and hardest things we have to learn. It's good to be able to read the signs, but they're easier to read if you know the alphabet.

At the last service of this chant series, this same person came in and sat down. Before she closed her eyes I called out her name and motioned for her to come over (there's a fairly universal hand signal for that). She did, we asked her our questions, and she sat down again. We played the best of the series of services for a couple of reasons: (1) We had the information we needed to feel secure in the form; and (2) we were able to pray for the first time because we weren't worried about monsters behind our heads, or distracted by incomprehensible hand signals. That communication is one of the most important steps required in order to feel comfortable and confident enough to perform well and pray well with others always comes as a shock to me, but nevertheless, it always comes. I've concluded that it's not unreasonable to expect someone to speak with me when I show up to lead a worship service. I'm not so self-important as to expect the red carpet rolled out, but it's a church—shouldn't I expect to find hospitality there? Lesson No. 8: I have the responsibility to ask for what I need, and it's easier to do that if I can focus on the task at hand, and not on the actions of the other people involved.

Chanting helps me to focus on what is really going on. Practically speaking, this means that I may learn a chant, but unless I use it—take it into myself, let it have its way with me and shape me—I am not taking care of the ground, and the hole is not worth the thirty bucks. Sometimes we just need to plant things deeper than we think.

Getting back to the garden metaphor: It's hard to think of myself as both the sower and the seed. This parable has had a big influence on me:

"Listen! A sower went out to sow. And, as he sowed, some seed fell on the path, and the birds came and ate it up. Other seed fell on rocky ground, where it did not have much soil. And, when the sun rose, it was scorched; and since it had no root, it withered away. Other seed fell among thorns, and the thorns grew up and choked it, and it yielded no grain. Other seed fell into good soil and brought forth grain, growing up and increasing and yielding thirty and sixty and a hundredfold." And he said, "Let anyone with ears to hear listen."

—Matthew 13:3–9

I try to picture myself as the seed, God as the sower. Through the grace of choice, I can decide where I'll grow. I may toss myself onto the path, overextending myself, and then nothing can get in. I am sometimes really dense. I am sometimes one of the people who know but don't do. Or, I may be fine until the going gets rough, and then I give up. There's a knot in my stomach that shows up when the heat's on, and I have to take many deep breaths to calm myself down. Or, I may not be paying as much attention to my spiritual life. Bills, work, my desire for this, that, and the other thing—pretty soon I don't even see the need for a spiritual life. "I can chant tomorrow. I'm tired tonight, so I'll just watch a little TV"; or, "I didn't get enough sleep last night, so I'll just sleep on the train instead of chanting."

On my best days, I realize I am not yet the person I wish to be. I set out to be mindful and poke around for the most fertile ground I can find. Occasionally I find some. There is usually music there. I can feel positively fecund, so productive that I am sometimes the singer and the song all at once.

In the bookstore where I work, I see people rushing around trying to take care of other people, or trying to look like they're caring for other people, and it's pretty obvious that they're neglecting their own ground. In the process, they tend to overstep boundaries, and they become careless in their dealings with others. How do I know this? Because I'm not innocent either. I see this particular demon from both sides, and it's not pretty. When I'm having one of those days, I am short of patience, and if a customer is one of those needy, greedy type A people, look out. One day, a woman came in at closing time and asked me which Bible she should buy for a gift. I decided I'd be nice and began giving her what I thought was a short answer, but she stopped me in my tracks, tapped on her watch, and said, "I don't have time for this." I looked her right in the eye, and said, "And I don't have patience for that, so if you'd like to leave, we're closed, but if you want a Bible, you have to let me answer your question." It was not my finest customer service moment, even if I was somewhat justified. I did sell her a Bible, but not from that happy place called "for the love of God."

It's important to tend my own ground and be prepared so I can keep my head when I'm under pressure. I'm pretty sure this will take my entire life, considering my automatic response to the time-challenged lady. After the seed-sowing parable, Jesus goes on to say: "Let anyone with ears to hear listen! Pay attention to what you hear; the measure you give will be the measure you get, and still more will be given to you."

This is true also with chant. Lesson No. 9: The measure you give will be the measure you get.

Chanting has moved my energy in powerful ways. I also see the effects of chanting on others, whether they're just singing inside or making a racket outside their heads. Let me give you an example of how it works. When my uncle was in the hospital a few years ago for an angioplasty, the nurses were worried that his oxygen levels weren't improving a few days after the surgery. They were watching his monitors, and as they watched, his oxygen level rose to normal. A nurse came in and asked, "What are you doing?" He said, "I was just lying here singing in my head." She said, "Well, keep singing because your levels are great."

Oxygenation is crucial to circulation. It used to be thought that spirit lived in the blood, and its world was magnetic. Turns out that oxygen and hemoglobin have magnetic fields that allow them to work together. Medieval people thought that in writing with liquid ink and a pen, the spirit of the person was captured. Maybe that's why I still feel so much richer when I receive a letter in the mail rather than an e-mail. I open the letter and the letter opens me. If we sing with our whole spirit, we become a circle of transformation. I sing the chant and the chant sings me.

So Who Chants?

Every spiritual tradition uses some type of chant (and often many types) both to communicate with and to touch the Holy within. People of every faith sing their prayers. In the Jewish and Christian traditions, sound is a factor at the beginning:

> In the beginning when God created the heavens and the earth, the earth was a formless void and darkness covered the face of the deep, while a wind from God swept over the face of the waters. Then God said: Let there be light; and there was light.
>
> —Genesis 1:1–3

First God creates with the use of sound, but the wind is already there. Wind is pure energy, and it creates vibration. Sound is also vibration, and it creates energy. It's as if the wind creates the vibration out of itself, which creates more energy, and on and on it goes. Sometimes the "wind from God" is translated as the "spirit of God." The two-volume *New Century Dictionary* published in 1927, which I was given about twenty-five years ago, uses almost a page to define *spirit,* but the most interesting definitions are: "breathe"; "breath"; "wind or breeze (obsolete or archaic)"; "the vital principle in man, animating the body or mediating the soul"; also, "conscious, incorporeal being, as opposed to matter"; "a presence inhabiting a place or thing or having a particular character"; and, "often, the soul or heart as the seat of feelings or sentiments, or as prompting to action."

Wind or breeze may be obsolete and archaic to my dictionary (hmm), but in Hebrew, there's only one word necessary to mean wind, breath, and spirit: *ruach.* I learned *ruach* about twenty-five years ago, and since then, I can't think of one of its meanings without the others. Wind conjures up breath and spirit, conjures up wind, and so forth—it's all very free and blowing like a fresh breeze in my mind's eye. After I began chanting, I began looking up those words in other languages to see what they had to teach me. In Italian, the word for spirit is *spirare:* "to inspire, to blow, to breathe in." In Greek I found *pneuma:* "wind, air, breath, spirit, used in combination;" and a "current of air" (even the angels need air for their wings). In French it's *esprit.* In Japanese it's *seichin:* the first character means "purify and/or distill," while the second character means "God." In Chinese, it's *chi* (ki), "life's animating force and substance"; in Dutch we get *geist,* which means "ghost"; and, finally, in Sanskrit, the oldest language I've found, *prana* is the word that means "life force, breath, and universal energy." In many of these languages, the concept encompasses all aspects of life: physical, emotional, and spiritual.

> As the wind, which is one on entering creation,
> Conforms its own form to the form of each being,
> So also the One, the atman within all beings,
> Assumes all forms, yet exists outside.

> —*Katha Upanishad* 2.2.10

Imagine a cool breeze on a hot day, as opposed to a cold wind on a cold day. Imagine the wind at your back, or the wind in your face as you trudge along. The effects of each of these breezes on us are very different. The Gospel of John says, "The wind blows where it chooses and you hear the sound of it, but you do not know where it comes from or where it goes. So it is with everyone who is born of the spirit." The Ashiwi (Zuni) nation are a native people descended from the Anasazi and living in what is now New Mexico and Arizona. They see everything as being infused with spirit, including rocks and trees. They believe that all illness is due to our being out of balance with natural forces. They have chants for everything, and I'll share the simple Sunrise Call in chapter 6. The Dine (Navaho) people were the first people of Utah, and they are also a chanting people. A Dine ceremonial Chant or Sing takes from one to nine days and consists of sandpainting, chanting, and ritual in order to restore harmony and balance. A Dine chant follows:

> In beauty happily I walk.
> With beauty before me I walk.
> With beauty behind me I walk.
> With beauty below me I walk.
> With beauty above me I walk.
> With beauty all around me I walk.
> It is finished again in beauty.
> It is finished in beauty.

This uncontrollably transcendent, free-blowing, numinous spirit of God is what we'll be trying to apprehend throughout the rest of this book, and I will try to introduce you to chant as a way to befriend that spirit in your form so that you have a helping hand in noticing the beauty all around, while you're poking about, transforming your own thicket. Since you've come this far, I hope you'll be moved to try the chants for yourself, and then you'll find out what a sound practice can do for your life. A search on the Internet or in a library will turn up more information than you can imagine about every kind of chant. There are thousands of CDs you can buy filled with thousands of chants to listen to. But there is a difference between listening to someone chant and actually making those same sounds in your own body. There's a difference in the way the vibrations affect you depending on whether they come from outside or from within you. Chant can work wonders when applied intentionally. Here's what my friend Kathy has to say about it:

> There is no bad place to chant except in an elevator with people who might try to flee because they think you are crazy. I chant everywhere, sometimes out loud and sometimes in my being. Chant is energizing, relaxing, motivating, healing, and centering depending on how I use it. It is a doorway that connects me to the divine realm and reminds me I am always there. I use it to decrease the spasms and tremors multiple sclerosis brings to my left side and to open my spine so the infamous MS fatigue and weakness abate. It decreases anxiety and depression. It is one tool that allows me to communicate healing to others, either near or distant. It bonds me more deeply with others I chant with. However, it does not iron, cook, or clean—clearly serious limitations.

Sound touches our depths more than any of the other senses because it comes from the deepest part of us. It makes contact with us in a very physically intimate way, and in a sense it is exercise for our very molecules. Chanting takes us directly to our core, and changes it for the better. Chanting has also taught me that at our core we are made in the image of God, and each of us possesses a portion of that image (inconceivable as that often seems). This is what we're given to work with in our lives—it's our raw material. What we can develop from this incredible gift is what we have to offer both to ourselves and to others, as we take care to remember that each and every one of us is made in that same image out of the same raw material.

CHAPTER THREE

HOW TO CHANT: IN THE BEGINNING WAS THE SOUND

Sound is a very powerful force and, like any natural force, it can be used for good or ill. Sound can open us up and sound can close us down. For years, I would jump at the sound of a slamming door. Why? Because I had a cellular memory of an experience that was traumatic. It took me a long time to figure out that now it was simply the sound of a slamming door. It wasn't the shadow of a bad experience, unless I chose to keep reliving the experience.

Sound opens me up to the world in ways that are mostly inexpressible, yet it moves me to the core. I'm pretty sure that our paths in life are connected to the things that move our hearts, and I've realized that chant is the type of sound that has the capacity to move and transform me more than any other kind of sound.

I find much of the music around us calculated to manipulate us in some way, so I'm not surprised that chant does it, too. However, in a world where our society seems to be locked on the manipulation button, I have a responsibility to myself to understand how I am being manipulated. Beyond that, I feel I should have the capacity to manipulate myself into the life that I would like to be living.

I've spent years reading about God and telling other people what to read about God, based on what I've read and on what I can intuit that they're looking for. About ten years ago, I began to feel like I was going through the motions and someone else was directing my life. This someone didn't happen to be my idea of God, either. At about the same time, I started to find it difficult to pray in a meaningful way. My focus has always been on praying for others more than on praying for myself. I've always tried to let God sort that other part out, relying on "The Lord will provide …" Or at least I thought I did. The time came when I had to sort out what was my responsibility and what was God's responsibility in our relationship. Now there's a lifetime of work! I think I was just too scared of what I might find if I started digging too deeply. The funny part is that I was so scared that I blocked out how scared I was. So, to help sort things out, I started at the beginning. Little did I realize that this was the start of my preparation for an ongoing spiritual practice.

MAKING READY

Only that day dawns to which we are awake.
—Henry David Thoreau

Space has a spiritual equivalent and heals what is divided and burdensome in us.
—Gretel Ehrlich

The importance of having a place where you can just *be* cannot be overestimated. Set aside a time that you will be accessible to work on your relationship with God without distraction. I like to think that I'm always working on my relations with God, by being open to whomever she sends, but there's a distinction to be made in the time I'm available to be with others and the time I set apart for God and myself alone. If I can remember to treat God as a guest, then I make sure my house is in order to greet her. Although my room is sometimes a messy place, it's more important to make ready by creating psychic or spiritual space to welcome the conversation. It's also important that I feel safe, because the work often cuts close to the bone—either because it's hard to get to the bottom of the things I ought not to have done, or because I'm too impatient to let the things I ought to be doing come in their own time, to name only two of my demons. It's hard to get to the crux of the matter at hand and work through the issues sufficiently if I'm interrupted by the door or the phone. I try to remember that this is my spiritual life, and that my relationship with God will be reflected in my relations with everyone else, so I've got to pay attention, and listen up. In this place, this safe place, I can openly look at both the divinity within my heart and the not-so-divine, without fear. The more I chant, the more I find that my heart knows where to go next. I trust my intuition more since I've been chanting regularly, and my mind even quiets down sometimes. If it sounds as if I think the heart is smarter than the mind, I do, and it is. I am sure that there's a lot of light in my heart, while I still need a good strong flashlight to see what's in my mind.

When I decided I would chant in an intentional way and actually sat down in my room to do it, my heart started beating in my throat. Nerves again. It took me months to get to the place where I understood all of the things that I sound so sure about now. The reality is that, ultimately, it's me and God on my cushion, and that made me really nervous at first. I can still remember how my heart was pounding, because this decision to chant felt really important to me, and I didn't want to screw it up. However, it seemed obvious that I needed to address my pounding heart before I could do anything else, so I drew on an exercise

I often begin with in rhythm workshops to get everyone entrained. The first step in a heartbeat meditation is to get in tune with that beat. It worked like a charm for me.

HEARTBEAT MEDITATION

What I was seeking in this exercise was a fundamental spiritual awareness of the underlying things we all had in common. For me, the beginning was the heart. We've all got one, we can't live without it, and it is crucially important for a healthy spiritual life. On average, our hearts beat about two and a half billion times in the course of our lives. That's about seventy-two times a minute, which sounds a lot more manageable. Breathing was a close second, and we'll get to that in a moment. But first, the beat of your heart. For this exercise, you don't need anything except an intention to be present with your own heart, and an openness to what it can teach you about love. Random thoughts tend to arise as soon as we turn the corner and head for quietness, but don't be discouraged. Just take note of them and let them depart. If you're like me, you had no idea you did *anything* two and a half billion times in your life. Take the time now to sit with your heart. Listen closely to where it is leading you, and follow its pulse through the meditation.

Find a quiet place. Sit in a comfortable position, either on a chair or on a cushion on the floor. If you choose a chair, sit up straight and place both feet on the floor (posture matters). Place one hand palm up on your lap. Using your other hand, try to find your pulse. Start with your radial pulse. It's usually pretty easy to find, just below your thumb. Take your second and third fingers and place them in the groove toward the outside of your wrist. If you can't find it, don't worry, you're not dead yet. You can try to find your carotid pulse, which supplies blood to your neck and head, by running your fingers along the outside edge of your windpipe. The lub-dub sound your heart makes represents the closing of the valves behind the blood. Once you find your pulse, sit with it for a minute or two, breathing regularly and feeling the pump, pump, pump. Each and every one of us holds this small beat in common. Note how fragile we are. Life is precarious and random, and we are easily broken.

When you feel comfortable enough and secure in the knowledge that you know your own heartbeat, the time comes to join the community. Listen. We must know our own heart before we can share it with others. Listen again to the driving rhythm of your heart; take all the time you need. When you feel ready, use your voice to replicate it. Try it on an AH or OH sound, one sound per beat, one beat at a time. Don't forget to breathe. Make a nice sound, not just a grunting noise, but more like the kind of sound you'd like to make so that the people you love can recognize you and your heart. The kind of sound you might make if you thought it was safe enough to be on familiar terms with the rest of God's people. This can be tricky, because most of God's people are not trouble-free. The point is that this is about you and your heart, and about your taking the time you need to get to know yourself so that you can be comfortable trusting the presence of God in you—enough to be able to live life with an open heart. This is not about believing in God, or even about God believing in you. Rev. William Sloane Coffin once said that "faith is being seized by love." Imagine your heart opening like a flower, naturally reaching toward the source of love.

Find your pulse again. Sit with it while you breathe regularly and picture what it is like to open your heart to the people you love the most in the world, both known to you and unknown; those who have made it possible for you to be here now; all who have come before you. Sit with them for a moment, allow yourself to feel their support, and thank them for it by letting them hear your heart sound. Then, when you feel ready, and a little more comfortable and sure of your heart sound, enlarge your field of vision to include your neighbors, your favorite teachers, the people on line at the grocery store, the people who make you laugh, the people whose hearts are closed to you, the people your heart is closed to, the ones who've caused you pain, and the ones you've caused pain. This part can be hard. I sometimes do it in the shower so there's a steady stream of water to wash away the tears. Return often to your pulse and your heart sound, to check in with yourself. Take it easy. Even the people who have hurt us are fragile and broken in places. As for your heart, I once read that when a heart is broken open, it can hold the whole world.

This is one of my favorite meditations because you can bring to it anything that's going on in your life. I sometimes find myself checking my pulse at work, when I feel scattered and busy. It tends to calm me just by taking the time to reacquaint myself with my natural rhythm. Some days it's a very happy, thankful meditation. I sing on AH and all is right with the world. Other days it can be very difficult. Things sometimes come up unexpectedly. I cannot sing on AH to save my soul, and I move to the more contained OH sound. It's important to pay attention to what comes up. If it's something thorny, you might want to make an appointment to meet with it later on in the shower. Start slowly and try it out, and take it as far as you're comfortable taking it (or letting it take you). In a sense, this is an exercise in discernment, will, and surrender, so if the same things keep coming up, you might want to enlist help in dealing with them. None of the exercises in this book should be used as a substitute for medical care. Chanting is in many ways a great overall help and contributes to our well-being, but if you need to see your doctor or therapist, by all means go, Go, GO!

I have also used this heartbeat meditation with specific intentions. I'll pick one word and repeat it on each heartbeat for a few minutes. When I expand the meditation to use a word, it's mainly to manifest the quality I feel I am lacking at the time. I insert the word into the middle of the meditation and end with the last part of the meditation, opening to the enlarged vision of being in my place in the world surrounded by others. Words I use with the heartbeat meditation: love, peace, hearing, presence, now, care, calm, beauty, source, open, listen, play, flow, heal, awake, attend, one, being, ground, all, yes, soon, life, joy … These are just some of mine. Make a list of the words that resonate with you and keep it in the place where you chant.

NURTURING THE SPIRIT: THE BREATH

Breathing—we rarely think about it, because it's one of the seemingly effortless things in life. When we chant, we move energy through the use of our breath, but the energy also moves us. We make sound, which is capable of moving energy in powerful ways, whether it's a still, small voice or an avalanche. We inhale a breath, and, as we exhale, it is the sound of our spirit that vibrates in our bodies. Our ears hear this sound and turn it into energy, which feeds our brain, causing it to relax. When our brain relaxes, attention can move to our hearts. As our heart expands with each breath and we nurture the Holy in us, we begin to be able to tap into the locus of our inspiration.

BREATHING MEDITATION

This meditation is called hara breathing, and I like to do it at bedtime. I lie down on my back, inhale for a count of five, hold it for five counts, and exhale through my mouth for a count of five. The idea here is to breathe gently, no explosive exhales or violent holding, just nice, easy, deep breathing. Think down as you inhale, and let the breath go down to about three fingers below your navel, then envision a place about one and a half inches in toward your spine. This is the hara, or center of gravity. *Hara* means "belly" in Japanese. It is the place where our vital life force lives. Breathing down and through to this place brings energy to your entire body, stores energy for later use, and is especially good for the kidneys.

Try it now, even if you're sitting upright reading this book. Breathe in for a count of five. Lightly hold for a count of five. Gently exhale for a count of five. Repeat. If you find it difficult to maintain 5+5+5, try it by inhaling for a count of four, holding for a count of four, and exhaling for a count of eight. The exhale for this variation is twice as long to enable you to eliminate all stale air.

Do this each night for about five minutes or so and let yourself drift off to sleep. Practicing this type of breathing just before bedtime allows us to learn it without distraction. Then, whenever we practice it—standing, sitting, in the morning, noon, or whenever—we can recall the quiet depth and gentleness of the first time. It's about developing the ability to bring ourselves to that open place where we're made in the image of God and God is within us. There's a space of equanimity that we can go to, a place of balance that is unafraid of challenge or change, and knows all will be well.

I practice breathing because I have asthma. For years I was a moderate smoker, and it took me a while to quit. I can be dense, so I of course waited until I got pretty sick, and then the light went on. There is nothing like not being able to breathe to help you see the importance of breathing. We don't pay much attention to it, but breathing is affected by our routines and emotional circumstances. Conscious attention to breathing for a short time daily contributes to our energy, vigor, and overall health, making it easier to find time to chant.

HUMMING AND TONING

Listen far beyond hearing, and call the unheard.

—Lao Tzu

The voice is nature's most perfect instrument. It has a magnetism that other instruments have been trying to capture since the dawn of time. It can tell us many things about ourselves. It is our barometer: It encompasses the fountain of our emotions. It lets us know how we're feeling in general and gives us big clues as to our physical and emotional reality. It betrays our energy level—picture a little kid right before bed, crying in a hoarse voice, "I'm not tired!" It shows the attitude of our mind: honest or dishonest, sincere or insincere—"Oh, I'd love to, but ..." ("No way in hell!"). Whether we're thinking about our greatest dreams or our biggest hurts, it is reflected in our voice. One good way to keep your voice in shape is to hum. Listening to yourself while humming provides greater benefits. It's not only a quick way to learn how your voice lives in your body but another way to generate health and healing. The voice you've been given is a part of your gift to the world, and no one else in the universe has it. A ten-minute humming practice every day can help you feel how your voice works, so you can really understand your raw material, and make music that reflects your inner nature. Aristotle said that art at its highest level happens when you pay attention to your inner nature.

Physically, humming is a high-frequency sound that stimulates the inner ear, the tenth cranial nerve, and the vestibular system, which is the part of our brain that deals with balance and coordination. High-frequency sounds stimulate us and increase our energy, whereas low-frequency sounds (TV, airplane noise, and the like) decrease our energy. Humming helps to increase energy and stamina; improve clarity, focus, and reading comprehension; balance brain waves; and strengthen the immune system by increasing the number of our antibodies. That tenth cranial (vagus) nerve connects the ear to the lungs, heart, and stomach, as well as being involved with psychosomatic disease. Bonus returns on an investment in humming have been reported by people who practice ten to twenty minutes a day: They feel more grounded, more relaxed and calm, better able to cope, more connected to themselves, more immune to the vagaries of hormones—and it feels like an inner massage.

Spiritually, humming is a great way to prepare for chanting. It warms up the voice by getting the air moving, and helps me create the interior space to openly relate with God. I also use my humming time to set my intention. I don't always have an intention when I sit down to chant, but I often have one (or more) by the end of five minutes of humming. Sometimes, if too many things come up as I hum, there's nothing better to remind me that I'm *not* God than setting my intention to "be still, and know that I am God." *Buddha's Little Instruction Book* says, "To meditate is to listen with a receptive heart." I often hum with that as my intention. There's always the "Please keep my ego out of our way" intention, and the "Please let me notice when help arrives, in whatever form it appears." I'm sure you can come up with your own. I find my humming and toning time is the place for me to get down to business.

HUMMING

> And we must learn that to know a man is not to know his
> name but to know his melody.
>   —Unknown Asian philosopher

The first step to knowing your own melody is to hum and tone. To hum, put your lips together, push them out just a little bit, and begin humming. The reason you push your lips out a little is so that you can feel the vibrations nasally. Play with it for a second and you'll see what I mean. (Forget about looking pretty. Chanting takes courage!) That's it. Try humming softly in the shower; on the subway (no one will even hear you); while you walk or do the dishes. Almost any time is humming time, with the following caveat: My friend Don Campbell, author of *The Mozart Effect,* once told me a story about being on an airplane and encountering a lot of turbulence. He began to hum a little to calm himself. When he stopped humming, it suddenly became so quiet that it scared the other passengers, because they thought an engine had failed. It turned out he was humming a lot louder than he thought he was. He laughs about it now, but it wasn't his intention to scare a plane full of passengers in midair.

TONING WITH VOWELS

The following letters are probably familiar to you as vowel sounds: *A, E, I, O, U.* In Tibetan Buddhism, the Jewish mystical tradition of Kabbalah, and even the Norse Rune religion, the vowel sounds are considered sacred. Vowels don't get in the way of our individual religious traditions because we are so familiar with them. This makes them a good way to introduce the concept of mantra chanting. Vowels are like mantras in the sense that each sound affects the energy in a certain part of the body. Everything about humming specified above is also applicable to toning. The only difference is that with toning your mouth is open. Each vowel sound produces specific harmonics that have an effect on our physical bodies. According to the ancient sages of India (rishis), the vowels are sacred sounds, and each one can be equated with a planet. I've used a numbering system that begins at the bottom of the body and works its way up to the head. Later on, you'll find the same logic applied to the chakras. Begin toning with (1) and work your way up.

(5)	(I) EEE	head (Mars)
(4)	(U) OOO	mouth/nose (Mercury)
(3)	(E) AY or EH	throat (Saturn)
(2)	(A) AH	chest (Jupiter)
(1)	(O) OH	central body (depends on pitch), solar plexus (Venus)

AH is the most open vowel; it is felt in your torso and chest. My favorite chant to use with AH is Ma. It's what I call my mother, but even more important than that, it is a sacred sound signifying the Great Mother. When you sing Ma, picture a bright golden healing light, and breathe it in. Picture the light surrounding your heart and spreading upward. Pick any note at all, and sing it for a full breath. Ma............ Ma............ Ma............ Ma............ Ma............ You may also send it to a person or place that needs healing. Once, during a chant workshop, a woman voiced a concern for someone close to her who was in the hospital after a car accident. We joined her in singing Ma, directing our intention to the man in the hospital. The woman sensed his presence and felt much better by having had the energy of fifteen other people address her concern. Chant is often a small, but powerful, thing.

OH is more interior, but still open; chanting OH feels like you're holding a sound ball, very full and round.

EEE is a great sound for energizing the head; it's good after lunch, or as a pick-me-up when you're tired. Try it for a minute or two, on a fairly high pitch (but don't hurt yourself!).

EH is for the throat chakra and also for the pituitary and pineal glands. I find myself using it when I feel like I'm not being heard.

OOO is the most closed toning vowel; in me it lives in my throat and third eye chakra.

THE ENERGY OF THE CHAKRAS

The Godhead is like a wheel, a whole. In no way is it to be divided.... Every creature is linked to another and every essence is constrained by another.

—Hildegard of Bingen

We humans are huge bags of uncontrollable energy. Or are we? We are nothing without our bodies, and if we're lucky, we're nothing with them. Our bodies have more channels than direct TV or the largest cable box. Each channel is there to conduct energy to the next channel. There are seven major energy centers in our bodies called chakras. *Chakra* means "wheel" in Sanskrit. The position of the chakras runs up along the spinal column and each of them corresponds to the placement of the glands in our endocrine system. There are actually many more chakras in or near our bodies than what I've listed here, maybe hundreds (for instance, healers often use the ones in the palms of their hands), but I'll limit myself to the seven main chakras so we can chant some more.

Cell biologist Rupert Sheldrake says we are a nested hierarchy of vibrations. Think of Russian dolls, nesting one inside the other. This is what the chakras are like in your body. If we had to consciously control all that energy all the time, we'd be dead by now. Besides, the energy seems to do a fine job on its own. The object isn't to control it, but to direct it somewhat. I think of it as being a tune-up. In order to direct the vibrations, you have to know a little about how they work. They are located in what is called the "subtle body," which both fills us *and* surrounds us. The chakras are both physical—concentrations of nerve centers that control certain organs and activity——and energetic. Carl Jung called them "psychic layers, or localizations of consciousness up from the region of the perineum to the top of the head."

If you look at them as representing the path of individuation (how we grow to be ourselves), you'll see that study of the chakras can occupy at least a lifetime. For instance (I'll only give you one—the rest of the journey is yours to take), the root chakra is the beginning of the journey of consciousness. It represents earth, foundation, ground, and kundalini, among other things. *Kundalini* means "coiled" and is often used interchangeably with *prana,* or "life force." You could say the root chakra is the Hindu spiritual awakening process, and it's represented as a coiled snake. This is the place where all creative energy is located, but not yet tapped. That's the part we put in: Through meditation we awaken this potential energy, causing it to flow upward, connecting each chakra with the next, developing our souls and our capacity for self-healing. When the journey upward is completed and has reached the crown chakra, the kundalini is pictured as having seven heads rising out of one snake. This symbolizes that our growth has gone through all the levels and has integrated them into a whole—us. A whole us.

The chakras are often pictured as flowers with varying numbers of petals. This started with the Sanskrit alphabet, which has fifty letters, each on a petal that corresponds to a place on the chakra wheel. I won't explain them all, but the root chakra, muladhara (*mula* means "root," and *adhara* means "center" in Sanskrit), has four petals (four directions, four elements, four seasons …). There are also symbols for each chakra, and at the center of the root chakra symbol is the sign La, which stands for "earth." Above La is the symbol Om, and together they make the sound Lam, which is the seed syllable that activates the root chakra. "Huh, what's a seed syllable?" I hear you. Each chakra has multiple characteristics traditionally linked to it: syllables, notes, planets, gems, elements, glands, desires, and so on. Each one also possesses more ethereal but distinct functions (the throat chakra governs hearing—remember Dr. Tomatis and the monks in chapter 1?). The chart on page 47 contains some basic information, which I collected from various sources over the last ten years or so. Think of it as a quick tour, and you can explore the chakras in greater depth on your own. You might want to inquire about relations between the seven chakras and the Seven Tabernacles, the way they relate to the Sefirot (the tree of life in Jewish tradition), Teresa of Ávila's Interior Castle, or Matthew Fox's exploration of the chakras as the flip side of the seven deadly sins to see some Western mystical angles of interpretation.

Association	Root Chakra	Sacral (Polarity) Chakra	Solar Plexus Chakra	Heart Chakra	Throat Chakra	Third Eye (Brow) Chakra	Crown Chakra
(Pitch)	(C)	(D)	(E)	(F or F♯)	(G or G♯)	(A)	(B)
Sanskrit	Muladhara	Svadisthana	Manipura	Anahata	Vishuddha	Ajña	Sahasrara
Planet	Saturn	Jupiter	Mars	Venus	Mercury	Sun	——
Color	Red	Orange	Yellow	Green	Blue, Cobalt	Purple, Blue, Indigo	White/Golden Light Violet
Element	Earth	Water	Fire	Air	Ether	——	——
Seed Syllable— Bija	Lam	Vam	Ram	Yam	Ham	Aum	Om
Gemstone	Garnet, Ruby	Moonstone, Golden Topaz	Tiger's Eye, Citrine	Rose Quartz, Emerald	Aquamarine, Lapis Lazuli, Turquoise	Amethyst	Clear Quartz Crystal
Aspects	Grounding in this world—Creation, Gate	Opposites, Sexuality, Reproduction	Unification of Opposites	Being, Wholeness, Love, Compassion, Honesty, Tenderness	Speech, Hearing, Creativity	Clairvoyance, Precognition, Intuition, Telepathy	Seat of the Soul
Gland	Ovaries/Gonads	Adrenals/Spleen/ Liver	Adrenals	Thymus	Thyroid	Pituitary and Pineal	Pineal and Pituitary
Sense/Function	Sense of Smell, Taste, Vitality, Kundalini Self-preservation	Cleansing Function, both physically and for negative energy	"Butterflies," Digestion, Mind, and Emotion Link	Lungs, Immune System	Metabolism, Thoughts, Writing, Speech	Eyes, Nerves, Brain, Spiritual Powers	Transcendent Knowledge

BIJA MANTRA

In upstate New York, I led an intergenerational group with an age span of one to about eighty. I led the group through some warm-ups and the kids were restless but participatory, while the adults sat stonily. Some were really into the exploration, but some were clearly not going for the ride. I've always been of the opinion that you get out of something what you put into it, so I just kept on doing what I was supposed to do and after a time, the kids quieted down. I've never had so many children in one room sharing their heartbeat with adults. The adults all had normal boring beats, but God must be making children with arrhythmias from a very young age nowadays—very loud, funny-sounding, creative arrhythmic heartbeats. I loved it. The adults didn't seem amused. The chant that finally quieted the kids down was a simple mantra called the bija sounds, an exercise I use in the morning. I'll describe it as simply as I can.

Bija means "seed" in Sanskrit. There are lots of seed syllables in Sanskrit. The chakra bija mantras are the ones I use most often. Each chakra has one bija syllable associated with it. The purpose of the bijas is to move the energy up, making them a great chant to do in the morning. I am oh-so-not a morning person that I'll try anything that comes with a wake-up call. The bija sounds are also a way to keep track of what's going on in your body. If there's a pain somewhere, it usually shows up as a difficulty in making the sound that goes along with a particular syllable. Funny, that. The idea isn't to fix a problem, but to be aware of any imbalances that might exist. Pat Moffitt Cook, author of *Shaman, Jhankre & Néle: Music Healers of Indigenous Cultures,* once said that the bijas are a way to manifest the you in you. And Alan Watts said on his recording *Om: The Sound of Hinduism,* "The you in you is the same as the you in me."

The chant is a simple mantra beginning with the root chakra; each sound is repeated twelve times on one pitch. Then you move up in pitch either a half or a whole step (whichever you prefer), until you reach the third eye chakra, which is sounded three times: one long breath for each time. You then sound one long Om at the crown chakra; then you think a silent Om while focused on a spot about eighteen inches above your head. Beginning with chakra number 1 below, try them for yourself, and see what comes up for you. You may also meditate on or tone the bija mantras individually. The chakra chart will be helpful in that regard.

Pronunciation Key for the Chakra Bija Mantra

a is pronounced as the *u* in the English word *but*.
r is softly rolled or flipped (you will feel it in your solar plexus).
h is pronounced as the *ch* in *L'Chaim* or *Loch*.
Aum is voiced using all three syllables: ah-ooo-mmm.

Silence—focus above the head (Om)

(7)	Om	crown—merged with God (1 time long)
(6)	Aum	third eye/forehead (3 times long)
(5)	Ham	throat
(4)	Yam	heart
(3)	Ram	solar plexus (sun, light)
(2)	Vam	belly (atmosphere, water)
(1)	Lam	root (earth)

Whatever happened to the group of adults and children doing the bija sounds? When we were finished with the sounds, we had the usual question-and-answer period, and I asked what people noticed, if anything. We were sitting at round tables, so I went around to each one and asked, "How do you feel? What did you notice? Did you hate it? Like it?" Some of the responses came from the adults: warm, focused, more awake, a sense of community. One three-year-old was standing up and her head barely reached the tabletop. She looked me right in the eye with a big smile. I asked, "How do you feel?" And she yelled, "Comfy!" An adolescent girl of about twelve said, "I feel unified." When I finish the bija sounds, I often experience my eyesight as improved and also feel a sense of clarity, maybe of being more awake after I've done them than I was before.

I wasn't really moved by the bija sounds the first few times I tried them. I attempted to learn the bija sounds about a half-dozen times before I "got" it. The way the bijas move the energy up is to wake up each chakra from root to crown and tune them up. Most of the first half-dozen times I did them I was not in the mood, or not paying attention, or distracted by the syllables themselves so as not to be able to attach them to a chakra in my body. It sometimes takes a while to get past the intellectual part of my brain. Because I fancy I "know" something about chanting, I imagine that the chant information got in on the left side of my brain instead of the place where all the other tunes enter on the right. It's funny to think that the more I know about a subject the less I see and feel about it. (And I am not alone.) I watch for that now, because one thing I really know is that I don't know very much, and what I know about that is very little. I also realized that the first three people who tried to teach me the joy of the bijas were categorized by me as (1) intimidating, (2) egotistical, and (3) both (and a little mean). When I finally got past myself enough to just sing the damn sounds, the idea that I might be my own biggest obstacle began to loom large as something I needed to look at seriously. Perhaps I do hang around a lot of people who make me crazy—but then I realized it could possibly be me who was making me crazy, that I was choosing to be made crazy by my expectations and what I perceived as other people's limitations, and vice versa. Things got both better and worse, as God in her wisdom is fond of reminding me. I no longer had other people to blame for my attitudes. I've been working on that whopper for some years now, and I'm a little better at staying detached and less likely to let loose careless arrows of hurtful words from my tongue's quiver. I think it was the Prophet Muhammad whose soul flew out through his lips, and I like that as an image. One can only hope that it might render me mute most of the time, but, sadly, I fail at that. I do try, though, to be more thoughtful and reflective before I open my mouth. Sometimes it's okay, sometimes I get so frustrated that I clam up and sing Om Shanti Om (which you'll find in chapter 5) in my head to calm myself. At least I listen better, and I don't verbally beat up on people as often, for which there is much rejoicing of angels.

Now that you've got a couple of ways of becoming aware of how sound lives in your body, you'll be able to notice more about how your energy works and how you can cultivate the sound in you. Using chant as a spiritual practice will change your life, which means you'll need new chant tools to help you deal with whatever comes up. It doesn't matter if you are young or old, in years or in practice. By intentionally drawing close to the presence of God in you—because you are also the presence of God— by drawing closer to the presence of God in you (I really can't say it enough), you will be given the opportunity to grow into the person you wish to become.

Join me for the ride of your life.

QUIET YOUR HEAD AND HEAR YOUR HEART

I don't think of myself as being naturally drawn to silence, but since I've been practicing chant regularly, I've experienced lengthening periods of silence between chants. Many days I find myself beginning in silence and moving into chant. There's something about silence as a prelude to chant that makes total sense to me on an intuitive level, but I have no practical idea why. Maybe I'm still listening for something I haven't heard yet? I've come to consider this time in silence as a refresher course. Staying open to the possibility that things can be different than they are now—even the things I'm happy with—has led me to see things differently.

Have you ever had the experience of being in a worship service and accidentally going deeper than you usually allow yourself to go in a group of people, so that you find yourself being snapped back to "reality" when the music starts or someone speaks? When that happened to me, it was a big clue that I needed to make other time available to intentionally go to the place from which I kept getting snapped back, which I suspected was an aspect of reality I was habitually ignoring. Unless I intentionally make time in which to contemplate God working through me, see how it's working already, how I might be missing it, or how I might make more of it, especially in community, I feel like I'm not really all there when I'm in the community. I have a sense of trying to cultivate an awareness of my place in the world, but sometimes I need to be apart from the group in order to reflect on how best to be with them. It's like having a practical sense of mysticism. I love the whole idea of God's multifaceted nature, and how I might draw from those facets to benefit all that is good and cool in the community. God often has different ideas about how I can serve than I do, and many times our ideas are diametrically opposed. I don't know why this still takes me completely by surprise. My friend John recently told me he was going to start the process to become a priest. I asked him if he thought his life needed a new direction, or if God was being a pain in the ass. He said God was being a pain. I told him there was nothing he could do about it—when God gets like that, she will not let up. Even if you think you're in charge for a while, the time comes when you find out that you have not been behind the wheel of your own car.

CHANTS OF DEVOTION AND GRATITUDE

I looked up *devotion* in my dictionary, and the definitions that leapt out at me (for very different reasons) were "set apart by solemn or formal act; consecrate" and "earnest attachment to a cause; dedication." I think the main issue I have with the first pair of definitions is that they seem so vertical: just God and me on our little island. That seems so "top down," hierarchically speaking, while I think of devotion as a kind of "being with": something that should happen between creatures (you, me, the birds and the bees). I like the second pair because I can sense aspects of my life and practice. I highly recommend earnest attachments, but I don't think God requires our veneration directed at *her.* I think all signs pretty much point in the same direction: Love one another. Something a little more horizontal, perhaps. Doing the inner work that it takes to live from your heart springs to mind. Making people happy seems like devotion, too. When we dedicate ourselves to making each other happy, and when we live our lives in a way that makes it possible for all the other people to live and love and be happy, we make God. That's how it works. The more you love, the more God you get. The more God you give, the more God in you. Make love, make God. Of course, sometimes, people can be a pain, and our own baggage can be equally painful, which is why it's probably good to have God around to practice with (on?). However, God doesn't need us to show *her* how thankful we are, but to show others.

ADORO DEVOTE

Suffice it to say I am never going to be the poster girl for the piously devout. I've never really been a "get down on your knees and pray" kind of person. So, imagine my surprise when Adoro Devote ("Humbly I Adore Thee"), with words by Thomas Aquinas (the tune of which is either a Benedictine plainsong from the thirteenth century or a French chant melody from 1697—I guess nobody won that fight, or else we'd be "certain" about its origin), wrapped its tendrils around me and would not let go. It happened one day in 1979 while I was sitting at a piano in Ithaca, New York. I don't play the piano capably, but I sometimes sit at one with music in front of me and play one hand at a time to see what things sound like. Well, this day I must have had a hymnal in front of me, because I can only remember spending many more days at the piano with that hymn open. It probably took me months to learn it, but I did finally learn it, and it is now in my piano repertoire. Sounds impressive, doesn't it? My piano repertoire. Do not be fooled. I can play maybe five things on the piano, each having taken months and years to learn. The thing about this chant is that it never really let go. Once I started chanting regularly, I realized that this is the case with all the best chants. Even if I'm not singing them, they have the capacity to single-handedly wrangle their way into my consciousness.

I came to this particular chant in my typically ass-backwards way. A few years ago, I wrote a chant meditation for six voices called Med. No. 9 ("Number nine, number nine, number nine …": blame the Beatles—I'd never numbered them before). The texts were given to me when I'd uncharacteristically said I would write a piece of music for a gig. I'd never done that before, and I didn't know why it just came blurting out at that moment, but I'd said it, and so I thought I'd better give it a try. There were three texts. The first was "Be still and know that I am God." One day it just showed up in four parts, and then tunes for the other texts showed up: "In thee, O God I put my trust" and "I am the God that healeth thee" came as counter melodies to the "Be still" text. Now, I do not normally speak in English from the era of King James, and I thought about modernizing the words, but I just let it go, because the tunes had come so easily, and, at our house, a tune is enough to get you in the door. The gig went well and a couple of people asked for copies, which was gratifying. One day about a year later I was practicing the piano part to use at a gig, and Adoro Devote showed up right there in the chant and started singing along. Startled, I cursed, but that just woke the dog. It started up again, and just when I thought it was over, around it went again. It was sneaky, though. The way it fit was that you had to play the meditation twice through in order to finish Adoro Devote once, which meant that everything went s-l-o-www-e-rrr. Since slowing down seemed to be the whole point of singing something like "Be still and know that I am God," I gave up and said, "Okay, I hope you know what you're doing." I spent a week recopying the original chant as a seven-part chant, writing Adoro Devote at the top of the other six parts. I thought I was finished with it, and that God should be happy. I was, and I was sure she'd get the hint and let up on me concerning this devotion thing. I felt like saying, "I'm grateful, okay? Now leave me alone, and let's move on."

Here's Adoro Devote, so you can see how beautiful it is. You could sing it in hell and it might get you kicked out, it's so nice. Let it go around a few times and you'll find you're in a different place when you finish, interiorly speaking.

Adoro Devote

If God were normal, that would be the end of it, right? Of course right. But God is not normal. Have I said that already? I'm sorry, but don't forget it. If you learn nothing else from this book, remember that God is the biggest, quirkiest, and most persistent mystery you're ever likely to know, and there's not a thing you can do about it.

KOSI R'VAYA

A couple of years ago, a friend lent me a CD of devotional chants by Rabbi Shefa Gold. Shefa (which means "abundance" in Hebrew) is into ecstatic devotion and is a leader in the Jewish Renewal movement. I am hardly into ecstatic anything. My friend wanted me to lead one of the chants in a service. I listened to the CD and thought there were a couple of chants that were pretty good, so I wrote them down in my notebook. A couple of days later, one of them came back for a visit. The text for the chant is Kosi R'vaya, which means "My cup overflows" or "My cup runneth over." It comes from the Twenty-third Psalm, which is most people's favorite psalm, if they have a favorite psalm. The important thing to remember about the psalm when singing Kosi is how it comes to be that your cup overflows:

> The Lord is my shepherd, I shall not want. He makes me lie down in green pastures; he leads me beside still waters; he restores my soul. He leads me in right paths for his name's sake. Though I walk through the valley of the shadow of death, I will fear no evil, for you are with me. Your rod and your staff, they comfort me. You prepare a table before me in the presence of my enemies; you anoint my head with oil; my cup runs over. Surely goodness and mercy shall follow me all the days of my life, and I shall dwell in the house of the Lord forever.

Kosi R'vaya is a beautiful and simple three-part chant that works because each part builds upon the one before it in such a way that you feel as if you're on the ocean. Kosi R'vaya is the waves before and behind you, endlessly overlapping, creating a buoy effect. Buoys have an innate capacity to stay afloat that never ceases to amaze me, and Kosi R'vaya, I noticed right away, is crafted to take you to the door of your heart and sail right in on a current of gratitude. The movement of the waves in this ocean feels like something we have felt before, but the most important thing that I noticed while chanting it in a group is the quality of the silence it engenders after the chanting part is finished. It's as if we know we've been here before and would like to spend some more time in this place. It is the same quality that I've experienced after a congregation finishes chanting Adoro Devote. It's a deep calm, an all-embracing quiet harmony that can only be created by a group coming together. I think it comes from the group intention, and each person's opening the door of their own heart and going within to drink from the cup that God's filled there. It's like being able to feed each other because you've each been fed by what you needed, and vice versa. I think of both of these chants as big surprises, because somewhere in the middle of singing them, you become more open than you were before.

We chanted Kosi in the service, it was lovely, and I forgot about it, until the next time I sat at the piano to practice Med. No. 9 for a gig, and Kosi came right in, and it wouldn't stop. It was like a three-year-old: "Mommy, Mommy, Mommy, Mommy ..." "Why are you here?" I wondered aloud. I kept playing the chant pattern on the piano, and Kosi kept singing along, and I kept trying to ignore it, because "I'm practicing!" Kosi just kept on singing, trying to tell me something that I was obviously too busy to listen to. So, I stopped playing. I looked at the page of music in front of me. I was, as usual, late, and I should have been going. I looked at the page again. Kosi started up in my head. I looked at the dog lying at my feet, the only one who willingly stays in the same room when I'm practicing the piano. (That's unconditional love.) I thought maybe she'd know why Kosi came in, but she was sound asleep, with one ear sticking up, listening for something that might not be me. So was I. I looked at the page again. I realized that both chants were in the same key, D. I noticed that Kosi wanted to start first. I put my foot down and said out loud: "I am not adding another part to this meditation!" It was probably more like whining, "I can't write it over again—it'll kill me!" because it takes a long time to write musical notation out in a tidy manner by hand, and I am not naturally tidy in that department. I get tired of working and trying all the time, and I am often ready to give up, but that's when God has you right where she wants you. This time, though, we compromised. I ended up taking the progression from Med. No. 9, and the Amen from Adoro Devote, and arranging them as an accompaniment for Kosi R'vaya. I still sing it almost every day. It almost doesn't matter whether I sing Kosi or Adoro Devote anymore, because whichever one I choose, the other one invariably shows up.

When you sing Kosi, picture yourself with a table spread before you. It is a gift for you from God. The gift is you. The gift is God. Picture your heart as the overflowing cup, full to the brim with waves of love coming and going endlessly. That's devotion and gratitude, and in my experience, they're joined at the hip.

Kosi R'vaya

Rabbi Shefa Gold

The bottom voice begins, and repeats until settled. Middle and top voices join in one at a time.

There is no way of telling people that they are walking around shining like the sun.

—Thomas Merton

I occasionally start my day with the following intention: to walk out my door as if I were going on vacation. On those days I still go to work and to the same places I go every workday. But I try to see it as if it were my first time (or the first time this year at my favorite vacation spot). It's always been interesting to me that on these particular days, everything looks fresh and new, and all the people are cute. Beauty is all around, and things are easy and light. I call it vacation head. If you find it hard to muster, just picture your favorite place and try to maintain that feeling on your morning commute. Okay, try to maintain the feeling until you get out of bed. It's like the Monty Python guys sang: Always look on the bright side of life.

It's the same with chanting. If you come to it with a vacation head, which in this case is perhaps the idea that you'll be getting an inner massage, or maybe a nice new relaxation exercise, then the actual repetitiveness of it won't get you down but will feel like warm fingers kneading out the rough spots. Mostly. Sometimes if I chant at night, I just find myself nodding off. I take this as an important cosmic message: Go to bed! Lesson No. 10: Chanting is more practical than you think.

It is a bit of a paradox that the constant repetition of a pattern can help to eradicate our tendency to fall into patterns, but such is life. Chanting is an effective way to keep me mindful of my moods and their effect on my feelings about all external things and beings. Why chant, besides its helping to keep me mindful? Believe me, I need to keep the mindfulness alert out in my life, because by nature I'm a space cadet who withdraws into whatever is most interior. I continue to chant because it feels good. I continue to chant because it feels good even if I feel bad. Whether I'm sick, crabby, tired, driven, scattered, or focused into a stupor, chanting can energize me in a way that no other form of prayer can. Chanting takes me to a grounded place where I feel content, as close to a state of equanimity as I've ever been; it calms me in tense situations; it helps me to be here now; and it feels good and real. Chanting helps me to be still, shut up, and listen beyond my mind. It's my main way of honoring all that I've been taught by the gods, and of nurturing that part of me that can be the kindest I can be.

I haven't always been intentional about it, but for the last couple of years, I've been chanting at least five days a week. On the days I don't chant, I still make sound, and I find myself with chants in my head much of the time. It's as if I'm training to "pray unceasingly" (1 Thessalonians). The chants spin around my brain through no effort of my own; it's just the nature of chanting: Once you turn them on, they keep going. Then you just have to renew them every once in a while, and they'll be your noisy little fruit-bearing friends forever.

I've been afraid to open my mouth about a lot of things in my life. I'm trying to overcome my fear through my chant practice. What this means is that I tend to take both the fear and the chants out with me; bringing chant along helps me to see the positive side of the fear and not react to it in the same old ways. If I fear a loss of connection, I listen deeply to try to hear what is being said and not shut down the pathways that help us to connect. That, in a sense, is gratitude. I really am grateful for a lot of things, and I'm sure, if pressed, each of us can come up with a long list. This is a good idea—try it. Make a list, and add to it whenever you think of something new or forgotten. Then put it in a place you can find, and chant it out loud on the bad days. Pick any note at all. I find that remembering to sing out my heart helps to quiet my head.

It hasn't always seemed important to be able to see my reality represented in the world (especially if I'm fearful!), but one thing I've realized through chanting is that I am often the only one able to capably represent my reality in the world. This has taken a long time to understand, and I can still hardly believe it some days, much less appreciate it. It's much easier for me to appreciate other people's reality than for me to respect my own as having some importance. Still, it doesn't negate the fact of Lesson No. 11: Your voice is unique in the world, and what you do with it is your unique gift to the world. Since we can't all have a Thomas Merton waiting on the street corner to notice, we need constant reminding, so here's Lesson No. 12: No one can do you justice like God shining through you.

This shining extends to all sentient beings. One night I was out in the park walking my dog Wanda, singing my favorite Kuan Yin mantra. We came around a corner, and there were three deer standing still on the other side of a low wall, eating grass, looking unfazed and beautiful. The dog looked up at me and started licking my hand, and all five of us just stood there. I tried to keep chanting, because that's what I'd been doing when we came traipsing around the corner, but as soon as I finished the repetition I said, "Hello," and fell into quiet, smiling at the deer, with them just looking at me, and the dog steadily licking my hand, occasionally looking from me to the deer and back. There wasn't a way to tell the deer that they were shining like the sun, or the dog that she was shining like the sun, but they were. I don't doubt for a minute that at that moment we were all on the same wavelength, and it seemed as if none of us wanted to move. For about five minutes we all just fell into our natural behavior, the dog happily sniffing away, the deer just standing there, eating grass and looking at us, and me open-mouthed and speechless.

KIRTAN

I enter the room and grab a cushion along the wall. I find an empty spot on the floor and join the semicircle filled with other humans, all sitting around on their floor cushions or mats, some sitting erect in full lotus (ouch!), some simply with their legs crossed, some folded over at the waist, prostrate in their devotion. Some have their eyes closed in meditation, others tune and play instruments: harmonium, tambura, flute, all kinds of drums. Some people dance. And everyone brings the instrument God has installed on his or her personal hard drive: a voice. That we choose to raise our voices is one thing. That we choose to raise them in a group of people, in praise and thanksgiving for what we've been given, in spite of all we encounter every day in our lives, is a miracle. The world is filled with apathy and manipulation and people I don't trust and weather I can't control, yet at the end of the day, at the end of the week, when I've finished dealing with the world and have a little time to myself, there's nothing like a good kirtan to remind me of how much God loves and fills absolutely everybody. It's like a free tank of gas: "Fill 'er up, please."

Kirtan (which comes from *kirtanam,* Sanskrit for "praise, eulogy") is a form of devotional singing common in India. It's also becoming more and more common here in the United States, especially in ashrams and yoga centers. Kirtan is a form of mantra yoga where the energy of the sound is focused on selfless devotion. There are other forms of mantra yoga where the sound energy is focused on sound as a word, a seed, a melodic progression, and the unvoiced, inner sound. Each form transmits a different energy. The words chanted (invoked) in kirtan are the names of God. We sing them in order to be joined with the qualities of the deity that we wish to embody. The actual singing is characterized by its call-and-response nature and its use of both melody and rhythm to praise God. What I like most about it is the form that most of the chants take: Starting slowly, everyone has plenty of time to learn the chant; then gradually the tempo is increased, arriving at a speed somewhere near ecstasy; then, suddenly, STOP! Whoa! Then, one last, long, slow repetition of the original theme, and the joyous silence of thanksgiving, peace, calm attentiveness, serenity, tranquility. The feeling it brings is very circular. God is in heaven, and all is right with the world. Krishna Das is a teacher and singer who leads some of the most popular kirtans in this country. Just one chant can easily last half an hour.

One of the most popular chants (even my eighty-one-year-old grandmother has heard it) is Om Namaha Shivaya. It means roughly "I honor the divine within." It is personified by Shiva,

God of destruction (the third God in the Hindu trinity along with Brahma [God of Creation] and Vishnu [God of preservation]). I've heard it sung to so many different tunes that I use a different one almost every time I sing it. When I'm at a workshop with my friend Ruth Cunningham, there's always a point at which we look at each other and say, "What do you want to do next?" Guess what text always shows up? Now we just laugh and say, "Om Namaha Shivaya!"

Pronunciation Key

Namaha (pronounced nah-mah-ha)
Shivaya (pronounced shee-vah-yah)

TAIZÉ CHANT

The Taizé community in France is a thriving ecumenical community with more than a hundred Catholic and Christian brothers from more than twenty-five countries. Founded in 1940 by Brother Roger, a Swiss monk, the community offered a place of prayer and shelter for spiritual seekers and also for refugees fleeing first from the German occupation in France and later from behind the iron curtain in Eastern Europe. Since the late 1950s, the Taizé community has been a place of pilgrimage for young adults. Groups from all over the world come to investigate the inner life through Bible study and chant, which the Taizé community practices together three times a day. Many churches and ecumenical groups in the United States have incorporated Taizé chant into their worship services. Although I've never been to Taizé, I've played much of the music, and there is a simplicity about it that invites everyone to participate. The form that it takes is accessible to young people because the instrumentation can include guitars, flutes, and pretty much any other instruments at hand. The liturgy itself is simple and the language the verses are sung in is often the language of the people in attendance. Since all languages are not created equal (some are harder to learn than others), Latin is still a very important element of the chanting. Latin was chosen because it's a "dead" language, one not spoken anymore. It was foreign to most young people, so everyone was on equal footing. However, the ease of pronunciation and the quality of the sounds created by the Latin vowels is unsurpassed as a way to access the power of our heart (see the Toning section in chapter 3).

My favorite Taizé chants are short, beautiful refrains sung in a repetitive manner. This makes them easy to learn and, as with mantra, the text is the medium that transports you past the world of words to the spirit the words are pointing to. The trick with repetitive things in general is that you have to let yourself get past the repetitiveness, a kind of letting go that happens when you chant through the boredom that sometimes tries to derail your train of thought. Only then will it take you for a ride. In a Taizé chant, the texts are more important than the tune. For instance, there are probably a dozen different Taizé settings of the simple text "Alleluia." *Alleluia* is one of the best words to sing. The long, open AH vowel at both the beginning and the end energizes our heart chakra. Many of these short phrases can be chanted on one pitch repeatedly. *Veni Sancte Spiritus* ("Come, Holy Spirit") is a good one to use on one breath, as is *Maranatha* ("Lord, Come!"), which is actually from Aramaic, and not Latin. The chanting of one word repeatedly is also characteristic of another mantra yoga (shabda yoga). See the resources section at the end of this book for information about music and recordings of Taizé chants.

CHANTING THE CHRISTIAN LITURGY

There are a lot of different kinds of chant that tend to be grouped under the umbrella term *Gregorian*. There's Ambrosian, for Bishop Ambrose of Milan (fourth century), which has the freest chants; Mozarabic, from Spain (there wasn't any Arabic influence in the rite, but there were Visigoths); Gallican, from France; Old Roman; and Antiochene (the Byzantine Rite is based on it). Gregory the Great didn't invent chant, and there's no proof that he actually wrote any chants. He was pope from 590 until 604 C.E., and he was credited with arranging the services of the year, the chants, and the liturgy in such a way that no one bothered to change his order for hundreds of years. This is actually a pretty big task to have accomplished, and Gregory was probably a huge control freak. I say this because, in the Roman Catholic tradition, there is a chant for every part of every thing that you could possibly imagine. Here's just a thumbnail sketch of the liturgy for Sundays:

THE PROPER OF THE MASS

These are the chants that change from day to day, whereas the chants in the next section (the Ordinary) remain fairly constant.

> The Introit—The chant sung so all the priests and their helpers get into the church; it clues the rest of us in as to what the topic of the day is.
> The Gradual—The chanting or reading of a psalm, usually with a refrain.
> The Alleluia—From the Hebrew word *Hallelujah,* it means "Praise the Lord." In addition to its place in the Mass, it was used throughout history for everything from a grace at meals to a battle cry. There are so many

different kinds of alleluias that they are sometimes
grouped by how many times you actually sing the word
in the chant: threefold, sixfold, and ninefold alleluias
are not uncommon.

The Offertory—The chant that is sung while we bring our
offerings to the altar (or they pass the plate), as the priest
sets the table for the reenactment of the Last Supper.

The Communion—The chant sung to cover the action
of people being fed bread and wine. This can sometimes take a while. Picture the feeding of the five
thousand …

THE ORDINARY OF THE MASS

The Kyrie—*Kyrie eleison* means "Lord have mercy." It
comes after the Introit.

The Gloria—*Gloria in excelsis deo* means "Glory to God in
the highest." It is sung before the Gradual.

The Sanctus—*Sanctus* means "holy" or "sacred." The
Sanctus comes after the Offertory and signals the
beginning of the Communion, or Holy Eucharist. The
text in English is "Holy, holy, holy Lord God of hosts,
heaven and earth are full of your glory, Hosanna in the
highest. Blessed is the one that comes in the name of
our God, Hosanna in the highest." In the Jewish liturgy
it was "Hosanna to the God of David."

The Agnus Dei—the Agnus Dei is sung during the
Communion before the bread and wine are distributed,
and the text of the chant means: "Lamb of God, who
takest away the sins of the world, have mercy on us"
(sung twice), ending with "Lamb of God who takest
away the sins of the world, grant us peace."

In addition to these chants, there are prayers and hymns
added to the liturgy. There are fifty-two Sundays in the

Christian liturgical year, and six seasons: Advent (four weeks of preparing for the birth of Jesus), Christmas (twelve days of celebrating the birth of Jesus), Epiphany (seven weeks for the three Magi honoring Jesus, and for telling us what he did), Lent (five weeks of anticipating Jesus's suffering and death), Easter (fifty days of celebrating the Resurrection), and Pentecost (the coming of the Holy Spirit to the Apostles—which takes the longest to work through, sometimes twenty-nine weeks!). Then what? Do it all over again. Not everything is sung on every Sunday. For instance, the Gloria and Alleluia are traditionally not sung during Lent, a penitential season leading up to Easter. There's more, but I'll spare you. Are you beginning to glimpse why I think Gregory the Great must have been a seriously type A guy? There are only fifty-two Sundays. What about all those other days? We'll return to the Benedictine monks for a bit to see what the weekdays might look like.

The Benedictine Rule says that "nothing ought to be preferred to the work of God," and by "work of God" Benedict meant the liturgy. Liturgy is supposed to be the work of the people, and let me tell you, in the Benedictine tradition it is a ton of work. Remember those monks from chapter 1? I looked up a "typical" day in a highly regarded monastic community that still chants, and here's what I found:

5:00 a.m.—Wake up
5:30 a.m.—Vigils/Matins (The night office ending at the dawning of the sun, originally based on the Temple service composed of readings from the book of the law, Psalms, and prayers.)
Time for personal prayer and reading
7:30 a.m.—Lauds (named for the three "praise" psalms that end the office—148, 149, 150) There is a lot of Laudate-ing in those particular psalms, ending with "Let everything that has breath Praise the Lord."

More time for personal prayer and reading
10 a.m.—Mass (about an hour and a half long)
Work
1 p.m.—Sext (Originally sung at noon, when the divine
    light is fullest. Also the time when Abraham received
    the three angels and when Eve ate the apple—a time of
    fullness.)
Lunch—(Thank God!)
2 p.m.—None. "Ninth" hour was traditionally a time
    for private prayer for others and for the church. Sort
    of a late addition based on the division of the day into
    quarters.
Recreation, more work
5 p.m.—Vespers, the hour when the candles are lit and
    the incense is burned.
Time for personal prayer and reading
7:30 p.m.—Dinner
8:30 p.m.—Compline, the last gathering for prayer before
    bedtime.

What this means for us is that there have been composers
writing chants about many aspects of spiritual life for more than
a millennium—a wealth of material for our personal practices—
and if they lived in a monastic community, it looks like they
didn't eat any breakfast. Even if this looks excessive, all the other
traditions have at least the same amount of detail in their traditions. Its purpose here is to give us some ideas about how we
might practice if we were to attempt to externally dwell in continuous awareness. I approach devotion with a bit more detach-
ment, and a day job, so I tend to seek out the more fun and
internal ways to maintain continuous awareness.

I'm not going to dig any deeper into the rhymes and reasons
of Christian chant, because it's at least a book by itself, but if you
are so moved, there are some resources in the back of the book.

Before we leave here, though, I would like to share one more Christian chant. The Veni Creator Spiritus ("Come, Creator Spirit") is one of the most beautiful—and one of the few chants used by all the Christian churches (Roman Catholic, Protestant, and Orthodox). It seems everyone can agree about the importance of the Holy Spirit. They say her name is *Ruach,* and we all want the wind on our side.

Pronunciation Key

Veni (pronounced veh-nee)
Creator (pronounced cray-ah-tor)
Spiritus (pronounced spee-ree-tooss with an "s" like bliss)

Translation

Come Holy Spirit
visit our minds
fill with supernal grace
the hearts you have made.

Veni Creator Spiritus

PLEASE, HELP, AND THANK YOU CHANTS (A.K.A. THE PSALMS)

Two thousand years ago in Jerusalem, it would have been strange and probably disrespectful not to chant Torah in the congregation. It is still chanted today, using much the same

form. Chant brings order to the prayers, rendering them intel-
ligible in a way that speech without song can't duplicate. In the
Jewish and Christian traditions, the chants are there to convey
the meaning of the texts more than anything else. However
questionable I might find some of the sentiments expressed in
certain psalms ("O Lord, kill my enemies, blah, blah, blah …"),
the Psalms have been central in communicating aspects of faith
for millennia. When I ride the subway in New York City, I try
to peek at what part of the Bible people are reading, and usually
it's the book of Psalms. By the time of the Second Temple, the
Psalms were the hymnbook for liturgy in the synagogue. It's
been one of God's secret surprise gifts to me to write chants,
and I've been provided with a couple of beautiful tunes. I don't
write poetry, so I'm always reading poetry and prayers, with an
open ear, listening for the tunes that lurk within the texts. I
copy any texts that speak to my heart into a notebook. The ones
that really move me get inside and live there for months and
years at a time, like a favorite record. Well, the Psalms have
been like that. They've also been a big challenge to me, because
there really is a lot of kissing up to God that goes on. Every
other minute, the psalmist is putting his trust in God, even
though his spirit is growing faint. And even when the psalmist
is considering the works of God's hands, there often comes a
point where something happens, where the psalm takes what I
consider a totally wrong and ungodly turn. For example (and
God knows there are many), I'll just open the book to Psalm
143:10–12:

> 10 Teach me to do what pleases you, for you are my God; let
> your good spirit lead me on level ground.
> 11 Revive me, O Lord, for your Name's sake; For your
> righteousness' sake, bring me out of trouble.
> 12 Of your goodness, destroy my enemies and bring all my
> foes to naught, for truly, I am your servant.

They don't all go there, but so many of them do that it's no wonder we still have wars all over the planet. I think it's important to stay open to most of the Scriptures, though, because extraordinarily beautiful things pop out all the time once you're in a relationship with those words. But a discerning spirit is needed, or else you can take a wrong turn and end up living in verse 12.

The upside of sacred texts, including the Psalms, is that there are people out there, dead and alive, who sometimes express our sentiments better than we're able to express them. There is also some small comfort to be found in reading about the countless others who have screwed up before us. That God shows love for people at their worst, and that I can perceive God loving them, is sometimes a complete surprise. I think that's probably another good lesson.

The Psalms are still sung today to a great extent the same way they were ages ago, in alternation between a soloist/cantor and the congregation. It's called responsorial psalmody, and it mirrors the construction of the Psalms' parallel phrases, the second an amplification of the first:

> Bless the Lord, O my soul / and all that is within me, bless
> his holy name.
> Bless the Lord, O my soul / and forget not all his benefits;
> Who forgives all your iniquity / who heals all your diseases.
> —Psalm 103:1–3

Get the idea? Much like a call and response, this type of chant is still sung in many places on the Sabbath, as well as in armies and in sports arenas (perhaps not with these same words). Many of the great Christian cathedrals of the world were built according to harmonic principles in order to be good spaces for sound (unlike your office cubicle). This same form of psalmody was later adapted for two separate choirs and called antiphonia (meaning the "octave"). *The Harvard Dictionary of Music* says that it "came to denote the singing of successive verses of a psalm by alternating choruses." Antiphonal chant was developed in Milan by Ambrose, a bishop in the late fourth century. It necessitated using a second choir, usually women or boys. One line was extracted from the body of the Psalm and repeated after every couple of verses; "His mercy endures, forever" is a popular one. Another way of singing the Psalms is commonly called organum. *Organ* means simply (or not so simply) "organ." What it mostly means to a musician, though, is a chant that has at least two parts, the root and the fourth or fifth sung in parallel.

Parallel Organum

Schola Enchiriadis (c. 850)

CHANTS THAT MAKE YOU MOVE—
WORK AND WALKING

The Five Books of Moses (called the Pentateuch, or Torah) are filled with stories that use chant in ways we don't usually hear about anymore. In the book of Numbers, at some point while the people of Israel are wandering around in the desert for forty years, there is a need for a well to be dug. The elders call the people together by chanting a promise: "Gather the people together and I will give them water." Then the people sing a work chant:

> Spring up, O well!—Sing to it!—
> The well that the leaders sank,
> That the nobles of the people dug,
> With the scepter, with the staff.

—Numbers 21:17–18

Unfortunately, our most obvious experience with work chants today is from *The Wizard of Oz* or a sports arena. Luckily, work does still seem to go faster when the stereo is on.

SA TA NA MA

Besides work chants, we have walking chants. One of the most powerful mantras, Sa Ta Na Ma is used in kundalini yoga and the Sikh tradition, as well as the Breathwalk program—a method for managing the use of the breath while walking in order to revitalize body, mind, and spirit. Sa Ta Na Ma is a catalyst for change in your life. The sounds of the chant are said to be primal, and they represent the following:

Sa—All that ever was
Ta—Creativity
Na—Destruction
Ma—Regeneration

I was taught that Sa Ta Na Ma is a monotone chant. However, one day in the studio I heard it at a slow 4/4 cadence in quarter notes, repeating fa-mi-re-mi-fa-mi-re-mi.

I have also heard it as a monotone whisper: Sa Ta Na Ma, Sa Ta Na Ma, Sa Ta Na Ma, Sa Ta Na Ma (four times). As a walking chant, it is very sticky—once you install this one, it will come back often when you're walking. It also works at almost any tempo, from very slowly, so you can reflect on time moving in your feet, to pretty quickly, so you can walk blocks in what seems like the blink of an eye. Each of these seed syllables can also be reflected on by itself.

OM SHANTI, SHANTI, SHANTI

Om is said to be the sound of creation, and it is said that you should always begin and end a lesson with it. At the beginning of a lesson, chanting Om helps to focus on the teaching. At the end of the lesson, we chant Om so we can retain what we've learned, and to invoke peace. It's partly a question of listening, but goes beyond listening to the words to being able to discern the spirit behind them. *Shanti* means "peace" in Sanskrit. It's a dynamic kind of peace, the kind of radiant peace that makes more peace.

Even though this is actually a very powerful peace chant, it is also an excellent walking chant, simple to learn and very powerful. This is the chant you want to bring with you when you travel to Washington, D.C., or anywhere else for a big march with miles of walking.

You might envision each "Shanti" as moving out to envelop wider circles of peace: individual and collective. My friend Ruth Cunningham told me a story about this chant. She was performing in a concert with frame drummers Layne Redmond and Tommy Brunjes, and it was just as the U.S. government was going to war with Iraq in 2003. As Ruth described it:

> Layne wanted to end the program with an Om Shanti chant with the audience participating. So I gave the audience the job of chanting Om Shanti, Shanti, Shanti in the traditional rhythmic tune and pattern. Over the top of that ground I started improvising using the words, Om Shanti Om, Dona Nobis Pacem, and Shalom. Audience members joined me, but there was a very strong core of Om Shanti, Shanti, Shanti going throughout, backed up by incredible Middle Eastern frame drumming from Layne and Tommy. It was very powerful and went on for a long time. The next day I was walking to my church job. I realized that Om Shanti, Shanti, Shanti was continuing to repeat as I was walking. I actually physically felt the mantra in the soles of my feet and I still do to this day when I bring my mind to it. For me this brought new meaning to the words "Peace is every step."

Vietnamese Buddhist monk and peace activist Thich Nhat Hanh has written a book called *Peace Is Every Step,* and in it he teaches that peace and happiness aren't things you need to wait for but are available to us all right here and now. He also teaches us how to cook potatoes.

Pronunciation Key

The *o* in *Om* is like the *o* in holy.
The *a* in *Shanti* is like saying AH.
The *i* in *Shanti* is said like EEE.

Om Shanti, Shanti, Shanti

Om   Shan - ti, Shan - ti,   Shan - ti____

CHAPTER FIVE

INCLINE YOUR EAR AND PRAY LIKE HELL

Most days I feel as if a monkey is running round my brain, so when I set out to accomplish a task, there's always a way to be distracted. Sound familiar? It's time to sit down to chant or write ... "I think I'll get a glass of water first, call my mother, walk the dog, start the laundry"; "Oh, look: time for lunch," and so on. It is always possible to fill up your dance card with activities that will not assist you in realizing your intentions. Yet we still cling to them, or allow them to cling to us, because they are familiar and comfortable. Ultimately, they don't feed us, but still we cling, because they are easy and not a drain on our energy reserves. Or are they? It dawned on me one day that the household tasks and errands, even though productive in one sense (clean laundry and a walked dog), were in a real sense contributing to self-neglect by being the enablers of avoidance. The daily round is often filled with obstacles that seem to keep me from getting to my real work.

Lesson No. 13: It is sometimes the things we wish for the most that we are most afraid of obtaining. Chanting exposes my predisposition to avoidance and is a healthy and pleasurable way to practice love of self and neighbor. It assists in maintaining energy and focus, and it feeds my spirit instead of feeding the same old "whatever." That I know this about myself makes it much easier to keep God before me, and you before me as God, too.

INVOCATIONS

In a workshop, someone once asked if "all this" wasn't just using our imagination to avoid dealing with reality. It is using our imagination, but instead of trying to avoid dealing with reality, we're trying to create new ways of approaching it. I don't know about you, but I get stuck fairly often, and in those times it's crucial to have a tool close at hand that can conceivably free me from my trap by helping me discover a new approach to a problem. Of course, it's still hard to remember to use the new approach until I'm totally at an impasse. Which brings me to invocation. How do we invoke what we need for our well-being? How do we call things up from within? How do we call things to ourselves?

I find that it's best if you ask, but it's hard as hell to ask. I'm terrible at it. I forget, or I think people should just know to do the things I want. Duh. And it gets harder to ask if you've been turned down after asking before. But luckily or unluckily (sometimes both on the same day), we are the ones who bring the meaning to our lives. It comes from within, here and now, no matter what you may have been told. God may give incredible gifts, or just a few that we finely hone, but we're the ones out there with the sharpening stone day after day, grinding, sharpening, and polishing. The intentions you set today will be the intentions you live out tomorrow. How you pray is who you are, and who you may yet become depends on how well you can listen to that still, small voice within, and respond to its urgings. This means that whatever your passion is, it's time to start living like it's as important as you secretly know it is. Your passions may feed your soul more than they do your body or your wallet, but that doesn't make them any less important. They just require an inclined ear in this noisy world.

Figuring out your passions allegedly starts early in life with "What do you want to be when you grow up?" That's one of those questions to which I still don't know the answer, except I'd still like to be me, I think. Or, I'd at least like to maintain some autonomy about who or what I might be or do. Beyond that, I have no clue. I've never really liked the idea of a career, because this implies that you have one good idea at a fairly young age, hop on an airport walkway, and go straight to your destination, with very few opportunities for exit along the way. A career runs you right through life, and I always stop and smell the flowers. The fast track is usually my ticket to an ulcer. On the other hand, my vocations make me sick only when I forget to balance the two that I've got. *Vocation* was once described for me as what we call up or call down—our voice. I like this image. It's a much better fit for me than *career*. Balance is the key, but how do we find and keep the balance? Trust me, it's easier to find than to keep. Chanting keeps me balanced by reminding me of the important things I tend to forget about in the rush to "get stuff done."

Sometimes chants seem to work by magic, and it is possible to summon to ourselves what we need. The Huichol Indians use *cantare* to mean "shaman," and I read somewhere that it originally meant "to produce by magic." *Cantar* is the Spanish verb "to sing." Being mindful of our true nature and our inclinations, asking for what we need, and listening closely are a few of the courses at the banquet of wisdom. Believe me, we are worth it. Besides, when we're hungry we eat and when we're thirsty we drink, right? So, how do you call your form of the Divine to you? When I'm surprised or stretched to a point where I need instant access, I often yell "Hey!" It started as a joke, something my grandmother says when she wants you to stop what you're doing and pay attention to her immediately. Usually it comes in threes, a trinity of "Hey!" The writer Anne Lamott uses "Help" and "Thank you"—also in threes. There are more complicated formulas, of course, and clearly more reverent methods, but it's really a very short trip from the Holy to us.

One summer not many years ago, I spent a week in a tent next to the ocean on the end of Long Island. It was early September (hurricane season), and the weather was feisty. We were happy to be evacuated from the area only once, at the beginning of our stay. I brought a copy of Marcia Falk's *Book of Blessings* with me to the beach that year, and I found myself on a very interesting threshold. I spent a good part of the week reading a novel out loud with my partner, Susan, and during our breaks I read through Marcia's book, with some manuscript paper in my lap. The wind and the surf were so much more powerful than usual, and I wrote a number of chants that week. There was no escaping the incredible power of reality when all that was between me and the breath of God was a thin nylon tent. It's hard to live on the edge all the time, with fifty things always pressing in, but on the beach, trying to empty myself and let Mother Nature do her thing, I experienced fullness and emptiness at the same time. I listened to the waves every day for hours and hours. I sat by them, stood at the edge of them, wanted to be them, then realized I already was. While I watched God lap at my feet and tasted God as salt in the wind, God flashed like fire by day and sailed by as moon by night.

There was a lot of radiance that week. I was kept awake a few nights by the relentless breathing of the ocean, and the flapping of tent walls in great strong winds. Do you know the feeling you get when you walk up to the edge of the ocean so you can feel the cold water and sand between your toes, and then you find yourself being drawn in a little further, maybe up to your calves, and then, Whoosh! God comes along as a big wave and you find yourself soaked up to your butt? God's funny like that. My spiritual director calls it "falling into the lap of God." Water, especially an ocean, reminds me how close we are to the Divine, and how close the Divine is to us. In and out, back and forth, over and under, not content to let us keep our distance. Of course, I can't spend my life at the beach, so I've had to develop some skills to get me to the place where I can tune in and be receptive without the need for fifty-mile-per-hour winds.

LISTENING

Our hearing is quite selective. The psalm says that God's ears are open to the cry of the righteous, but I can't pay attention to some people to save my soul. Why is that? I think we all have this problem to a certain extent. We hear what we want to and block out what we don't want to hear. Sometimes it's because the sound is unimportant (the hum of the refrigerator), other times because we're tired or overextended, still other times because we're closed to whatever or whoever is in front of us ("I will not learn from you" is one manifestation of that). Sometimes we hear things when we're closed down that we interpret based on how we feel, rather than on what's being said by the other person— because, face it, we interpret everything through our own special set of lenses that may or may not be clean—and the other people are speaking to us based on how they're feeling. They may be afraid to say whatever it is, or may feel intimidated by us, or whatever; and we hear the anxiety, fear, and the like as being directed *at* us, when it may have nothing at all to do *with* us.

Listening is hard work. It is discernment in the sense that we make decision after decision as to the meaning of the content put before us, and everyone and everything put before us is different! Couple this difference with the fact that our brains love patterns, to the exclusion of reality more than we'd like to admit, and listening becomes next to impossible. It's a miracle that we can communicate at all.

By listening not with the ear but with the spirit, one can perceive the subtle sound. By entering into that sound, we enter
into supreme purity. That is why so many religious traditions pray, sing, or chant as a prelude to silence. They understand that the repetition and absorption of sound leads to
sacredness itself. The deepest sound is silence.... Silence is
sound unified with all of its opposites ... and it is in this con-
fluence that the power of meditation emerges.

—Deng Ming Dao

CHANTS FOR PEACE

By now you've tried the chants and exercises in the previous
chapters, and you are under sound construction along with me.
In the next two chapters, I'd like to introduce you to more of my
sound friends. I've arranged the chants topically so you can find
them when you need to invoke them. I'll start with chants for
peace because war is a huge problem crying out for creative solu-
tions the world over, and the first step toward peace in the world
is finding it in yourself. Peace chants help me to listen more
attentively and make me more receptive when I can't bring
myself to listen. Making peace within is my greatest challenge.

OM SHANTI OM

This first chant illustrates chant as paradox: Three little words take
us to a place far beyond words. It's another Om Shanti chant, but,
unlike the previous one, this one's like hopping the express train to
the interior castle. It's simple to learn, and it transcends our regular
wordy brain in less than five minutes. The power of this chant is
not to be underestimated. It brings peace of mind and deep relaxation, which makes it easier to hear the reality behind the patterns.
There is a quietness of spirit that overcomes me when I finish that
connects me to a new frame of mind, one where I can really listen
and hear. There is something inexpressible yet very healing about
it, and it's one of the most soothing mantras I've learned so far.

Focus on the third eye chakra (because Om is its seed sound) and think "radiant peace." Then chant for three to five minutes, or until it's finished (chants have a life of their own and tend to end themselves). Chant one Om Shanti Om on each breath. Make sure you engage your whole body when chanting this one. Don't keep "Shanti" all at the front of your mouth. Try engaging your solar plexus for the "sh." Take a deep breath and sing. It doesn't need to be loud, but it should feel full.

SHALOM

Fullness brings us to Shalom. *Shalom* means "Peace be upon you" in Hebrew and includes a sense of wholeness. Shalom is one of the names of God. In an earlier chapter I pointed out how the Jewish and Christian traditions have much in common in terms of history and practice. The Jewish and Hindu traditions also have much in common, mostly on the playground of the mystics. Shalom and Om Shanti affect the same place, vibrationally speaking. I feel a sense of complete harmony in my heart chakra when I chant Shalom. Shalom has much to recommend it, as you will find out soon enough. Sound the notes sol and do, ascending, a half-note on "sha" with a good "sh"— send it out there to the open "ah." Sound "lom" until you run out of breath, but make sure you close onto the "m" for a couple of beats before you finish. Repeat for five minutes or until it's finished.

DONA NOBIS PACEM

Dona nobis pacem is a Latin phrase meaning "Grant us peace," and it ends the Agnus Dei portion of the Mass. We usually make up a new chant for this in every workshop, because something has always just happened in the world to make everyone anxious to ask for peace. Sigh. The thing I've noticed, though, is that both Shalom and Om Shanti usually come in at the same time as the Dona Nobis Pacem. I think it's great because that way people can pray the one they need. I also like the idea that Dona Nobis Pacem is asking for peace, while Shalom is giving a blessing of peace and wholeness, and Om Shanti is bringing peace of mind. I often find myself improvising on "pacem." All in all, it's a very satisfying experience. Shalom, Om Shanti, and Dona Nobis Pacem have a very healing effect overall, and as we go along, you'll notice that many of the chants and mantras serve more than one purpose. Let your intuition guide you.

MANTRA

Before we go any further, I'd like to explain a bit about the nature of mantra. Mantras originally were passed down from teacher to student, and the knowledge of them was tightly held by the Hindu Brahmin (priestly) caste. But we live in the Internet age, and there are so many mantras out in the world on their own that we can put to good use that I would be remiss if I didn't give some basic information about them. Besides, they are a big part of my practice. I'm just a beginner in the use of mantras—I've only used them for about three years. There is so much more to learn that I encourage you to follow your heart, your intuition, the resource list in the back of the book, and your Web browser if you want more information. *Mantra* comes from the Vedic *man,* meaning "to think," and *tra,* meaning "to free or protect." Thinking takes energy, and all mantra is about energy. As you've no doubt noticed from the chakra bijas, Sanskrit mantras are energetically empowered sounds crafted to change us. After all, all our prayers aren't going to add an ounce of holiness to God—we say them to make ourselves more holy. The Sanskrit language was built upon vibration. Each of the fifty letters represents an energy. It is called the language of the gods *(deva-ani),* and the written form *devanagari* means "city of the gods." Sanskrit is considered to be the mother of all tongues and is Indo-European or Aryan in origin. It was used as a literary language but is now, like Latin, considered a dead language. It never ceases to amaze me how many obsolete dead things seem so alive and full of spirit.

In chapter 3, we got acquainted with the chakra bija mantra. Next we'll add the foundation bija mantra. You've seen three of them before: Aum/Om, AH (big release), and Ma (healing sound and the syllable of the Great Mother). As you can see from my attempt at a simple explanation of Aum/Om, one syllable can open entire worlds for us to explore. For instance, each of the letters that make up Aum/Om can also mean waking, dreaming, and sleeping. It's a mystic's delight. The interpretations are endless.

Mantras are helpful in neutralizing and dispelling negative emotions, promoting inner alignment (check out the chakra chart again!), and helping us to rid ourselves of the patterns of thought that blind us to reality. There is power in thinking a thought, and power in saying a thought without thinking about it, but the science of mantra was built on the premise that the most powerful utterances are the ones we make while thinking about them. There are mantras for treating specific ailments, removing obstacles, finding a partner, ensuring protection, and more. There are short seed mantras, and longer chants that are mantras. Think of it as sonic spirituality—using our voices so that we can consciously direct our energy to achieve inner balance and alignment. The sound tools of mantra are very specific and it's best to say them correctly to affect the right energies, so I've provided a Web link at the end of the book to enable you to hear audio files if you cannot read music (and even if you can, it's always nice to hear things once or twice).

There are four traditional ways to use mantras. The three ways to recite or intone them are by saying them out loud (vaikhari), by whispering or softly humming them (upamsu), and by mentally reciting them (manasika). The fourth way is to write them down (likhita). I was taught that it's best to begin using mantra out loud so that you can hear and feel the vibrations. I often chant on the train, either humming or silently, but when I'm home, I chant out loud. If you find yourself drifting off, try switching forms. Silent repetition is said to be the most powerful, but if you find yourself overwhelmed at any point, stop for a little while and then go back to it. When I first began chanting, I found myself having to stop for a bit almost every time I began a new mantra cycle on the train because I felt like there was too much vibration going on inside. I think we just need time to get used to the mantras, because our bodies need time to adjust to the extra vibrations. I've always been able to go back without any trouble, sometimes in a few minutes, and sometimes in a day or so. Be gentle with yourself, and listen closely to your body.

CHANTS FOR HEALING

Every faith contains chants for healing. We all need them at some time or other. I've found that learning them before we need them is a good idea. Next we'll take a whirlwind tour through some well-known bija mantras. I'll list the mantras and their characteristics, and then you can refer back to the list at will. There are many more than those listed, but I've limited myself to healing mantras I have known and loved. Remember that seed syllables represent qualities more than the meaning of the letters that comprise them, and the way we get to know them is by using them, noting the nature of each syllable as we work with it and it works in us. Understanding the meaning of a particular mantra is important, but not all mantras have an English translation.

Each of the following may be chanted on its own or associated with its Hindu deity in its longer form. All of the personifications in the mantras are aspects of God manifest as a type of energy. They are symbols of sound. These deities have been personified because it's easier for us to understand things that are like us. These are the most basic mantras, the foundations upon which more complicated mantras are built. What I do is to try out each of the syllables for a couple of days, for five minutes or so. If I feel comfortable (and if it sticks), I move on to the longer mantra. I usually do a forty-day cycle of 108 times a day (sometimes twice a day) for each mantra that "speaks to me." We'll take a long look at Aum/Om, so you can get an idea of how deep we can dig, and then we'll move on energetically.

AUM/OM

Traditionally, Aum/Om is the prayer that even the gods use to address the Holy One. It is called the *pranava mantra,* "the source of all mantra." As a symbol of the Supreme Spirit, broken down into its three component sounds (a-u-m), it represents creation, continuance, and cessation (like the Hindu trinity mentioned in chapter 4). Aum/Om is the primordial sound of God. It is the sound of creation, blossoming, and closure. It is a holy sound. I'll try to explain it as simply as I can. In addition to the information presented in chapter 4, Aum/Om is used at the ending of the recitation of sacred texts and some Buddhist devotional services. You will find it at the beginning of many mantras. It brings energy to the third eye chakra by joining the male and female energy flow.

A is the first letter of the alphabet in the language you are reading. In Hebrew, the first letter of the alphabet is *Aleph*. In his *Book of Letters,* Lawrence Kushner points out that *Aleph* doesn't have a sound, but it is the sound that you make before you make a sound. He goes on to note that it is the first letter of the first of God's names, *Elohim,* and the first letter of the fact that "God is One," *Echad,* among other things. Think of it as the sound of a baby's first breath—the inspiration—Ahh. Christians know it as the first letter in the word *Amen,* which is often translated "So be it," and which *Aum/Om* also means; *Aum/Om* and *Amen* also both mean "yes," as in our assenting to allow the unfolding of God's will for and in us. In Tibetan Buddhism, the *A* stands for the essence of the Heart Sutra. The beginning of the Qur'an has it written as *Alm,* but the *l* in Arabic is pronounced like a "u" if it comes before another consonant. Anyway, once the *A* has become, it needs to be able to continue. Simple enough? On to the next vowel.

U symbolizes preservation, and, indeed, when we sing it, *U* is a very contained sound. If we were to sing nothing but AH, we would expend all our energy, and then we'd be very tired. So we move to *U* because creation needs preservation in order to evolve. The Qur'an says that first there was the word *be* and then there became. Becoming is good. The *A* and *U* can probably go merrily along together without end, except for one small problem: Humans tend to run out of breath. Ultimately, all things must come to an end. Which brings us to the *M.*

M brings us home to ourselves and brings with it the cessation of sound. This Aum/Om is a very circular sound—first we send the *A* out from us, then we try to catch it and hold it, and then we begin again. The Padma Purana says, "The syllable Om is the leader of all prayers; let it therefore be employed in the beginning of all prayers."

A NOTE ABOUT ENDINGS

Many mantras have one of two endings. *Namaha* means "I offer" and isn't gender-specific. The other ending, *Swaha,* is associated with the celestial plane. If you are twenty-eight years old or younger, Namaha is used. It vibrates in the lower chakras because that's what's being developed at that age. Swaha is used most of the time if you are older than twenty-eight. This is because our energy center moves up as we age. If the ending changes, you'll see: "Namaha (Swaha)." There are times, however, when Namaha is retained no matter what your age. Then you won't see an option. Just use the appropriate ending and you're on your way.

AIM/EIM

Eim (pronounced I'm) is the sound associated with wisdom, language, education, spiritual knowledge, music, and all things artistic. Saraswati, a feminine principle (and Hindu deity), represents how this energy is called to us. The foundation mantra for Saraswati is Om Eim Saraswatiyei Namaha (Swaha). The rough translation for this is "Om and salutations to the feminine energy that enlightens all artistic and educational endeavors, and for which Eim (I'm) is the seed."

DUM

Dum (pronounced doom) is the syllable associated with protection and helps in overcoming fear. It is a feminine energy represented by the goddess Durga, whose mantra is Om Dum Durgayei Namaha. This means "Om and salutations to the feminine energy of protection, of which Dum is the seed." The Durga mantra has serious energy. If it doesn't feel suitable, stop doing it. That said, Durga clears energy by wielding her sword of truth, and she will cut the illusion out of your life. This mantra removes spiritual barriers. One friend uses it at work to protect her from the people there who disturb her balance.

KLIM

Klim (pronounced kleem) is the energy of attraction, of calling something to yourself. It's personified by Krishna, eighth avatar of Vishnu, and central figure of the Bhagavad Gita (Song of God), an episode in the Mahabharata. Krishna is also big on the Dance of Love *(rasa-lila),* and he is often depicted playing the flute. He was all about devotion and loving service to God, and he is called the Supreme Lord of the Divine Love. A favorite mantra for attracting love is Om Klim Krishnaya Namaha, which means "I attract the principle of divine love in the form of Krishna and offer salutations."

SHRIM

Shrim (pronounced shreem), the energy of grace, beauty, abundance, love, and health is personified by Lakshmi, whose mantra is Om Shrim Maha Lakshmiyei Swaha. As many times as you chant this mantra is how many times more abundance you'll be able to attract and keep in your life. Shrim is also the seed for a mantra made up entirely of seed syllables: Om Shrim Shriyei Namaha (Swaha)—a powerful mantra for finding new approaches for healing, by helping to open up a new perspective. The Lakshmi mantra roughly translates "Om and salutations to that feminine energy that bestows all abundance, and for which Shrim is the seed."

GUM/GLAUM

Gum (pronounced as the English word *gum*)/*Glaum* (pronounced glah-owm) is the seed for Ganesh (Ganapathi), son of Shiva and remover of obstacles. This mantra removes blockages between the root and third eye chakras. You've seen this energy represented as the elephant-headed god. The mantra Om Gum Ganapathayei Namaha is known to remove all kinds of obstacles. Done with your partner, it can help clear the energy from misunderstandings. It's good for overall healing, because removing obstacles makes room for other things to come in. This mantra translates as "Om and salutations to the remover of obstacles for which Gum (Glaum) is the seed."

RAM

In the chakra chart in chapter 3, you'll see that Ram (pronounced rahm) is the bija mantra associated with the solar plexus. Here's a mantra for taking advantage of the healing energy of the solar plexus that usually lies dormant in us—Om Ram Ramaya Namaha (Swaha). I was taught that it is especially good for relieving physical pain and easing mental suffering. For those of you who don't know Rama, he was Prince Rama, the seventh avatar of Vishnu, and an honorable and brave soldier. He was married to Sita, for whom he searched the world over when she was abducted by the evil Ravana. There's a modern retelling of the Ramayana by Ramesh Menon that is a most beautiful way to become acquainted (see the resources list, p. 150). We don't have a lot of masculine energy around our house, and there are certain qualities personified by the Hindu avatar Rama that I need in my life but do not naturally possess, so I call them to me by virtue of this mantra. The first time I ever chanted it, I experienced the feeling that somebody was watching my back, in the sense of protection. When I do it now, I feel safer, as if I have 360-degree protection. It's as though I can see in all directions with clarity of vision and feeling. There is also a heat that builds up in the middle of my back at the level of my solar plexus (maybe from all those rolled r's). This is an excellent supportive and grounding mantra. Before reciting Om Ram Ramaya Swaha, I was told to visualize perpendicular lines (two lines that intersect to form four right angles, like this + with a garnet at the center. The garnet symbolizes passion, vitality, and purifying of the blood. After a forty-day cycle, I feel healthy, ready for anything, and aware. I repeat this one regularly.

Om Ram Ramaya Swaha

Om   Ram   Ra - ma - ya   Swa - ha

CHANTS FOR DISPELLING FEAR

Even though the darkness is not dark to God, it gets pretty damn dark down here, so there are piles of chants and mantras for overcoming fear. Many traditions use what I call good luck charms, to ward off evil and bad luck, to help us to be less fearful, especially at night. There's a Christian prayer from the Compline service that says, "Guide us waking and guard us sleeping, that awake we may watch with Christ, and asleep we may rest in peace." The Lord's Prayer asks, "Deliver us from evil." Jesus is seen as being powerful enough to convince demons to run into pigs and off a cliff. Most of the time, though, fear is an internal condition, and internal conditions need to be dealt with internally. When I'm fearful, I need a way to call up God in me right away, because sometimes the voice of fear within me gets louder than the voice of God. People use medals of saints, rosaries, prayer wheels, even blessings to keep all the bad stuff at bay. (Once, when I was having a hard time with someone, a nun told me to pray that God would lead him to better things in far-off places, which reminded me of the blessing for the czar in *Fiddler on the Roof:* "May God bless and keep the czar … *far away from us.*")

In the Jewish tradition, there is a small container called a mezuzah that is hung in doorways. Inside the mezuzah is a handwritten prayer called the Shema, a section of the Bible that reminds us to love God, just as God loves us. In Hebrew it reads: *Shema yisrael, Adonai Eloheynu, Adonai Echad.* Rabbi Lawrence Hoffman and Ron Wolfson, in *What You Will See Inside a Synagogue,* translate the Shema as, "Hear, O Israel, the Eternal is

our God, the Eternal alone." What a great way to remind ourselves that God is in charge. The Shema is traditionally said at
bedtime, and according to *The Complete ArtScroll Siddur,* "The
recital of the Shema immediately before retiring is perceived as
a protection against the dangers of the night *(Berachos Sa)*." In
the siddur, or prayer book, its context is as an invocation, at the
beginning of a bedtime service with psalms and prayers. It's said
out loud with the right hand covering our eyes, while we reflect
on how God is god and we are not. Since God is on the job, we
can sleep tight. For the longest time, I thought the most important part of this phrase was "God is One." Lately, I'm looking at
it from a different perspective: We'll never get to the One if we
can't hear, and that can't happen unless the people actually listen
to the One. This has proved harder than you might think for
many millennia.

BUILDING THE CONTAINER FOR SPIRIT

I was standing in the front of the church, in the middle of Holy
Week. The sun was setting and the light was growing dimmer
by the minute. We were chanting—improvising and listening.
Six men were surrounding the congregation singing Psalm 143

in plainsong. I looked up from my book while I was holding a long note, because I felt something happen. Something bigger than normal. As I lifted my eyes, I saw a man, about halfway back in the congregation, drop his head into his cupped hands. I tried to look at other faces, but there were too many eyes looking back filled with tears. I quickly looked at the surrounding chanters. Their heads were bent to their books, but there was something different about the sound. They were *really* connected. They had been connected before, and they had sounded great, but this was different. Now it seemed like cords were strung from one to the other, each voice crossing over every other voice, as if someone were drawing a star across the room with a pencil. The men were all breathing together, but it felt like everyone in the room had the same breath pattern. Most important, though, they were being sung. We were all being sung right through by something electric. I'd intuitively decided to do this psalm in a new way earlier in the day. I'm a firm believer in taking something that I know really well and doing something completely different with it, based on an inkling (that still, small voice). That night, something opened in all of us and God came shining through. I mean shining.

I put my face back down into my book before I lost my place and wondered if anyone else had noticed the change. Afterward, one of the chanters came up to me and said, "I saw a white light go right across the church during Psalm 143." I mumbled something about how I'd felt it, too.

I thought about it the whole way home, through two states. I thought about it for weeks afterward. We build these containers that look like churches, synagogues, mosques, kitchens, circles of fire in the woods, and we try to get closer to God by going to them. But I think we're genuinely surprised when God shows up. For people to feel free enough to let God be, they need to feel held and supported. We've given that job to a building, but I think it's not enough. There need to be people in the building who are willing to hold and support the group, so I'm sometimes moved to picture myself extending my arms around the room and embracing everyone in it, cradling the space. The rest is up to God. I'm just supposed to sing. Psalm 143 is a melancholy kind of a psalm, beginning with "Hear my prayer, O Lord; give ear to my supplications in your faithfulness; answer me in your righteousness."

I wish I'd been able to say what I knew about that light at the time. I know that all of us must have been united in our asking for what was in this psalm, and the energy of that unity created favorable conditions for getting an answer. That night it looked like a white light, but it was speaking to people in whatever way they needed to hear.

A Tibetan Chant to Open the Mind

Padmasambhava is a Buddhist saint. He converted Tibet to Buddhism, and he is considered the father of all four Tibetan Buddhist sects. He was a scholar, magician, and meditator (not necessarily in that order). This is a very sticky mantra, in that it goes right in and starts spinning after about a dozen repetitions. (Of course, that could be because I needed it when I found it.) The Padmasambhava mantra is called the mantra of transcendent knowledge, and it has no real translation (I guess if you have transcendent knowledge you don't need a translation). It is a chant for removing negative energy because Padmasambhava can subdue all demons. It is also for pacifying the mind by opening us to enlightenment and new ways to act wisely.

Pronunciation Key and Definitions

Om a hum (pronounced om-ah-hoom) in this case is more conceptual and can mean "body," "mind," "speech," or "our whole selves."

Vajra (pronounced vah-j-rah) means "thunderbolt" and represents enlightened mind energy. Roll the *r* and it will sound like three syllables with a hard *j*. This is right.

Guru (pronounced goo-roo) means "wise teacher."
Padma (pronounced pahd-mah) means "lotus" and calls
    the compassionate nature of enlightenment.
Siddhi (pronounced sidd-hee) means "accomplishment."

The Tibetan pronunciation is Om Ah Hung Benza Guru Péma Siddhi Hung (pronounced om ah hoong ben-za goo-roo peh-mah sidd-hee hoong). There are a number of mantras that have different pronunciations in Tibetan because the Tibetans found the Sanskrit syllables hard to pronounce. Either version is okay for chanting.

Padmasambhava Mantra

Om A Hum   Va-j-ra Gu-ru Pad-ma   Sid-dhi Hum

THE POWER OF WORDS AS ACTIONS

Speech is priceless
if you speak with knowledge.
Weigh it in the scales of your heart
before it comes from the mouth.

—Kabir

I understand all too well the power of words. Because words (like *spic* and *dyke*) have often been used in the past to hurt me, I know a little about their importance. We grow up thinking that it's okay to say something that we don't really mean. This is fine, as long as we can convince ourselves that we haven't done anything wrong because we didn't mean anything by our words. Remember the playground chant "Sticks and stones can break my bones, but names will never harm me"? It is completely untrue, yet we still use it and teach it to our children to make them feel better in certain situations. Can we please stop doing that? Here's one reason that goes right to the point, from the vast store of Persian wisdom: "A gunshot wound may be cured, but the wound made by a tongue never heals." Well, maybe not so long as *never,* but it can easily take decades. Our words are actions, and they often have unintended consequences of which we may or may not ever be made aware.

Try to remember how you feel when someone mispronounces your name or says it in an unflattering way. Even this seemingly small thing has an effect on the way you see yourself, on the person who says your name in a careless way, and on the energy in the room. It can make you less likely to open up and share deeply, or to let your true self shine through. It might even make you feel that your light is not as bright as the light of other people you know or admire. Different aspects of our personalities are called out of us by the way we are addressed. So, I spend the first few minutes of almost every workshop listening to each person's name and speaking it back to her or him correctly. You can see when a person expects the name to be a problem for others—she becomes smaller, kind of muted. It's as if she feels less significant or feels that you think of her that way. Likewise, when you take the trouble to say a person's name correctly, she seems to sit straighter in her chair, and sometimes the person emits a radiance that sparkles.

The first chant that I can remember learning and taking to heart was the following: "Ana banana plays the piana, all she can play is the Star Spangled Banner, Ana banana split!" It was often used by my peers to convince me to go away. Off I would go, with it ringing in my head on repeat for hours sometimes. Not a pleasant experience. Luckily, I found another rhyme and used it as an antidote. I would chant "25 Pandora Drive"—the address of the house I grew up in. My rhyming address held all the magic of Pandora's box. Remember the myth of Pandora?

She was given a box by Zeus, but he told her not to open it (silly god!). She grew more and more curious, she opened the box, and all manner of evil and misery flew out to afflict humankind. But it wasn't my curiosity that caused the box to open—it was my despair at being treated badly, so I thought it would be okay to do it. I imagined the lid exploding open and all the evil and misery in it coming to my aid. That worked for a little while, but not for very long, because although I felt protected, I didn't really want to hurt anyone. I just wanted them to stop taunting me.

Then, when I was ten, Martin Luther King Jr. and Bobby Kennedy were murdered for what they were saying. That had a profound effect on me, and after I devoured every newspaper article I went to the library to read more about them and other people like them. King quoted Gandhi, so I read Gandhi. I read everything I could find then (and since). What I gleaned from that year was the knowledge deep in my bones that I was a pacifist. Knowing how it would possibly work its way out in my life was another mystery entirely. I remember reading about Gandhi's mantra, and hearing it from a friend, but I obviously wasn't ready to really hear it yet. I never imagined that I might feel protected by—of all things—a mantra. About three years ago, I came across Gandhi's mantra again in a book by Thomas Ashley-Farrand called *Healing Mantras*. (There's a link to a sound file on his Web site.) The mantra is called the Rama Taraka mantra, and it is practiced by orthodox Hindus to attain liberation from rebirth. It was given to Mahatma Gandhi by his nurse when he was a boy. On the day he died in 1948 he was heard chanting the name of Rama. This mantra and the next are also liberation mantras, in the sense that if you practice them they will take you across the ocean of samsara (the phenomenal world), and you will no longer need to be reborn in this realm. The Rama Taraka mantra roughly means "victory to the spiritual self."

Pronunciation Key and Definitions

Sri (pronounced shree) means "master."
Rama (pronounced rah-mah)
Jaya (pronounced jah-yah) means "victory" or "success."

Rama Taraka Mantra

Voice

Om Sri Ra - ma Ja - ya Ra - ma Ja - ya Ja-ya Ra - ma

A LIBERATING CHANT: ASHTAKSHAR MANTRA (THE SACRED EIGHT LETTERS)

This particular chant, Sri Krishna Saranam Mama, comes from an esoteric collection for Brahmin priests and devotees of Krishna, and it's part of a worship ceremony (called a puja). The mantra has eight syllables and each has a symbolic meaning. With drums and flutes, this really rocks, and it's just as satisfying when done alone and unaccompanied.

It means roughly "Krishna is my shelter."

Definitions

Sri (pronounced shree) brings wealth and good fortune and is associated with Lakshmi, although normally *Sri* means "master."

Kr withers and destroys our previous sins, clearing our karma.

Snah drives away misery and misfortune.

Sa liberates you from the sorrows of birth, death, and suffering.

Ra gives you divine knowledge of the deeds and form of the Lord.

Nam causes steadfast devotion to Krishna.

Ma brings eternal love for Krishna.

Ma means you will obtain unity with Krishna, who will be your companion until eternity, and you'll never need rebirth again.

We've covered quite a lot in this chapter, and don't worry if you can't take it all in. It's taken me years to learn, and I'm still taking it in. I feel as if I learn something new every twenty minutes, and that's okay. I encourage you to explore the chants that speak to you, use the Web links and check out different types of chant on the CDs, and open yourself—mind, heart, soul, and mouth—to bring chant into your daily life.

CHAPTER SIX

LISTENING BEYOND HEARING

Prayer isn't always easy. I'm glad to be able to chant my prayers, because I don't always know what to say—the world is filled with an unbelievable array of problems, some people's blessings are other people's problems, there's too much to pray about, so many to pray for, and more stuff just keeps showing up. There are as many ways to pray as there are people. The important task is to keep the channels open to whatever is needed at any given time, but even with a list, I always forget someone or something. I've decided that the best way for me to pray for people is to increase my ability to be compassionate. In a way, it shields me from the despair that sets in when there are just too many things to deal with at once, when it feels like there's not enough energy in the world. But consciously increasing my desires to love and to be more compassionate somehow helps me to find the energy.

You can only pray what's in your heart.

So if your heart is being ripped from your chest
Pray the tearing

if your heart is full of bitterness
pray it to the last dreg

if your heart is a river gone wild
pray the torrent

or a lava flow scorching the mountain
pray the fire

pray the scream in your heart
the fanning bellows

pray the rage, the murder
and the mourning

pray your heart into the great quiet hands that can hold it
like the small bird it is.

—Elizabeth Cunningham, "Heart Prayer"

COMPASSION AND LOVINGKINDNESS

The Chinese Buddhist tradition is where I found my favorite mantra. Kuan Shi Yin is the feminine manifestation of Avalokiteshvara, a Buddhist god of compassion. Her name means "to see the sound." This is the one for me. It brings me right to the door of the Holy, the place where I find myself at my most permeable or transparent. It's like opening an interior door to the spirit I want to be: compassion. It's the hardest chant to sing well, but it doesn't matter, because this channel is all compassion, all the time. It's even taught me to be compassionate with myself—no easy task.

KUAN YIN

A couple of years ago, I played at a conference on domestic violence. When I drove up to the door to unload the car, I was
greeted by the sight of eight wooden figures on stands being
unloaded from the car in front of me. Each was a life-sized representation of a woman who had been murdered by her husband
or boyfriend. It was a sobering sight. No one knew quite what to
do with them, but it was clear they were supposed to be with us,
so after a while the eight figures were placed around the perimeter of the eighty or so chairs, encircling the living. I was off to one
side near the piano with my musical partner. It was our job for
the two days to hold the space so that the learning could take
place. When they arrived, the people would look at one of the
figures, read its plaque, and then avoid looking at the others.
T. S. Eliot once wrote, "Humankind cannot bear very much
reality," and this was surely a case in point. It became clear that
people needed a way to engage with the murdered women,
because the whole purpose of the conference was to learn how to
wrap your head around the issue in order to be able to respond
to it. There was a lot of left-brain activity and many presenters.
The wooden women surrounding the group made me feel as if I
were being held in the space. They were a visual representation
of all kinds of failed hopes, dreams, visions, and lives (not necessarily theirs). This gig was one of those times when I went in
totally unprepared in terms of what I would do to lead the
group. My main objective was to try to stay open enough to let
the energy flow through and aim it where it was needed.

The conference was organized as a Christian response to
domestic violence, but I could not get the Buddhist bodhisattva
Kuan Yin out of my head. Her long, traditional mantra wouldn't
stop spinning in my head. During a musical break, I introduced
the mantra, telling the group that Kuan Yin was a bodhisattva of
compassion, that a bodhisattva is one who delays her or his own

enlightenment to be of service to the rest of us, and that Kuan Yin is a protector of women and children. Then I asked them to hum with an intention to discern their personal response to the issue. The question that came to me was "How can you stay engaged?" I couldn't give voice to the question, even though it felt really loud, as if it permeated the air and all of us. There had to be a way to bridge the gap I perceived. As I stood in front of this group of people, surrounded by the eight wooden women, the idea of a walking meditation was given to me, and we were off. I asked the group to follow me around the perimeter of the circle, while I chanted the Kuan Yin mantra and played a guitar accompaniment. People slowly got up and followed.

I usually like to be on the margins of any given group; I'm the one you can find leaning on the back wall, watching the action. But for many people, the margin is a difficult place to stand. It's a kind of liminal space where anything can happen, and often does. It's difficult to be totally comfortable on the margins, and easy to be fearful. If you fear engagement because you don't want to share the fate of others, Kuan Yin is the one to help you get past that. Like Jesus, who was also big on compassion, she did some of her best work with the people on the margins. These eight women had already been more than marginalized in their short lives.

We alternated the Kuan Yin mantra with a simple Taizé refrain, "Ubi caritas et amor, Deus ibi est," which can be translated as "Where true charity and love are found, God is." I walked slowly around the circle. I stopped and read the plaque for each of the women while I sang, before proceeding on to the next one. It seemed as if it took forever, but everyone followed me. At first the energy in the room was very uncomfortable, but then the energy settled; something let go. It became easier to be in the room after the meditation was completed. Before the meditation, the eight were holding us in their space, creating a kind of container for the group, and the group perceived it as constricting. It was as if we couldn't appreciate what the women were doing for us because we were afraid to engage with them. I tried to act as a bridge for the group, by using chant to help us all confront the paradox of wanting to help yet fearing engagement, and I felt a release of negative energy.

Lesson No. 14: Sometimes the uncomfortable things in life need to be approached from a different angle. The chant served as a foundation, a constant that could be returned to: a touchstone, something familiar, guiding each of us around the room in an encounter with the stories of these murdered women, leading us back to the task at hand—thinking creatively about how to educate people and respond quickly enough to minimize domestic violence in the future. Sometimes chant can be the vehicle that encourages you to walk through the valley of the shadow.

After the conference, I found a story about Kuan Yin, about how she helped a man build a bridge. There are many incredible stories about Kuan Yin, but the main thing to keep in mind is that she can help you with almost anything but she only works with what is. Her power isn't magic. Fate can be changed for good or ill, based on the availability of compassion. The text for the mantra is Namo Kuan Shi Yin Pusa, and it means roughly "I call upon the bodhisattva who sees and hears the cries of the world."

Pronunciation Key and Definitions

Namo (pronounced nah-moh) means "to call upon" or "I take refuge in."

Kuan (pronounced kwan) means "look" or "see."

Shih (pronounced shee) means "world."

Yin (pronounced yinn) means "sound."

Pusa (pronounced poo-sah) means "bodhisattva, one who delays her or his own enlightenment to stay in the world and save others."

Kuan Shih Yin Chant

Traditional

Na-mo Kuan Shih Yin pu___ sa   Na-mo Kuan Shih Yin___ pu___ sa

Na - mo Kuan Shih Yin pu - sa___   Na - mo___ Kuan Shih___

Yin pu - sa   Na - mo___ Kuan Shih___ Yin pu - sa.

Rabbi Shefa Gold, the composer of Kosi R'vaya (see chapter 4), was doing a weeklong chant workshop at a college in the Hudson Valley. I couldn't attend the whole workshop, but was planning to go for one day. Time got away from me, though. When Shefa called me at work to say it was her last day there and that she'd like to meet me before she left, it was providentially just in the nick of time for me to catch a train from Manhattan home. Then I jumped into my car and chanted for the entire ninety-minute drive.

That morning on the train into work, I'd written down my experience with the Kuan Yin mantra and was wondering again how energy really works in a group. In the last couple of years, I'd had some really intense energy experiences in group situations using chant, but I didn't feel as if I had the words to explain them articulately. Most people have chant experiences in groups before they start humming the chants around the house, and they remember them as nice tunes or moving experiences, but there's not usually any planning involved in learning them. We go to church, synagogue, school; if we're lucky we meet a nice tune, it either sticks or it doesn't, and then we go home. Communicating about what happens seems pretty hit-or-miss.

As I drove north, the evening light along the Hudson River was so incredibly beautiful that I could have died happy. It was like looking at paintings from the Hudson River School. It was a privilege to be able to have a car, to know how to drive, to be able to drive on such a beautiful road, to sing beautiful music with beautiful people ... I was so mesmerized that I got lost. I arrived more than an hour late for the workshop, the last in the weeklong series. When I came in, Shefa was just about to introduce Kosi R'vaya to the group. That itself made me feel better than I normally would have about being late. It was a small group, but everyone sang well and we had three parts going in no time. We sang through a few more chants, and then Shefa gave us a handout called "Eight Functions of Consciousness in a Spiritual Group," describing with absolute clarity the roles, in terms of energy, that people must assume in a group situation. (Shefa later generously allowed me to include the handout in this book—see p. 110.)

My mouth fell open when I read her words, and I almost cried. Lesson No. 15: God is full of surprises, especially when you're not looking for them, and even when you think you're hopelessly lost. I hadn't planned to use the Kuan Yin story in this book. I wrote it because I had just lived through and written down the experience of chanting Psalm 143 and seeing the white light, and I knew the two stories were somehow connected, energetically speaking. I still didn't know the words to explain how. When I read that sheet and saw the roles of Container and Bridge, I nearly died of shock. Having outside corroboration for the fact that energy is palpable, and that it works in tangible ways, made me feel good. It turned out that Shefa has been trying to find (or create) a language with which to talk about energy since she was sixteen. The way she explained it that night is that all eight functions need to be present in a spiritual group in order

EIGHT FUNCTIONS OF CONSCIOUSNESS IN A SPIRITUAL GROUP

RABBI SHEFA GOLD

The Empowerer

Dedicated to the group energy; channels energy through themselves to the center of the group so that everyone can be nurtured and empowered.

Task: Building up group energy

The Guide

Sees and holds to higher purpose of the group, builds structure and plan; sees and nurtures the potential of the whole and the capabilities of each part.

Task: Perceiving guidance and steering the ship

The Observer

Conscious attention on behalf of the group; maintains awareness of group's energies while still being part of it; discriminates shifts without being judgmental.

Task: Perceiving the energy of the whole

The Container

Guardian of the group; creates safe/sacred space by containing the energy. Three methods—imaginal arms, heart, and voice; guards against outside intrusion.

Task: Protecting and embracing the energy of the whole

The Exalter

Raises up the spark of the Divine by seeing and celebrating it. Lifting the group by joyful presence.

Task: Loving whatever is Divine in this … exalting it, and bringing it out still further

The Foundation

Creating solidity, bringing grounding; laying one's consciousness beneath what is happening as a dance floor that supports the group's energies.

Task: Establishing the foundation for the group energy

The Secret Heart

Completely effaced in God/Devotion; the deepest part of the group, the least-known part to outsiders and to the superficial; God in the silence.

Task: Surrendering to the depths on behalf of the group, thus connecting the group with those depths

The Bridge

Making connections through interdisciplinary awareness; enlarging the meaning and the context for the group; bridging different states of consciousness and levels of meaning.

Task: Holding paradox, cultivating stereoscopic mode

for the group energy to be healthy and whole. We may be really good at one or more of the functions, and we may not be very good at others. We will often find ourselves fulfilling more than one function in any given group or doing more than one task at a time. Shefa later wrote to me: "I find that when people learn a language to talk about energy, then they can use it more consciously. I teach people to recognize and practice each of the eight functions, and then to forget about them, so they just become part of our expanded awareness."

Having the eight functions written down has been a great addition to my practice, and I should probably laminate the handout before it disintegrates. The way the language of energy came to me is a case of the generosity of Shefa, and of God listening to me better than I listen to myself. This happens a lot lately. I wonder about something, and then the answer shows up in an unexpected way, shape, or place. Don't get me wrong: I really do try to pay attention. But lately I get the answers before I even know how to formulate the questions. I don't have any more control over what happens, but I have a lot more faith that what is supposed to happen will happen. On the other hand, when I left the college chapel that night after meeting Shefa and the group, I was so tired from all the excitement of the evening that I got a speeding ticket on the way home. As I sat in the car waiting to be written up, I wondered if there was a way to describe the energy of the moment. Then I remembered the following meditation. It took a long time for the police officer to write up the tickets (turns out my license was expired, too), so I had time to make up a tune to go with it.

LOVINGKINDNESS MEDITATION
I first fell in love with the Mettabhavana (lovingkindness) meditation in Jack Kornfield's book *The Art of Forgiveness, Lovingkindness, and Peace.* It's a way of developing compassion, or *metta.* The lovingkindness meditation helps us to intentionally

expand our awareness of pleasant and unpleasant manifestations of energy and gives us a way not to get stuck in either of them. It has five stages, beginning with yourself: Start by finding and nurturing a feeling of lovingkindness in yourself, by using a phrase of affirmation (for example, "May all be well, and may I be happy") or by visualizing the light shining on you, enabling your heart to open like a flower (or you can do both). You can also use a phrase that states your aspirations for yourself. Use a simple chant—whatever comes to mind along with your phrase is fine. I find it's more powerful if I sing it out in the air, where I can physically hear it. Just remember that the idea is to stimulate the growth of your innate love and compassion. The next stage extends the affirmation/aspiration to someone you love ("May all be well with her and may she be happy"); then next to a neutral person (the pizza delivery guy, or the police officer who is writing you a ticket in the patrol car); and then think of someone you just do not like at all. Here's where it might be easier to think of the meditation as one of loving acceptance at first, because the point is to grow in love, which means it's time to replace your unhealthy and negative thought patterns with compassion—the other person's issues are not under your control. The final stage is to bring yourself and the other three people together and extend the *metta* out into your street, town, state, country, continent, hemisphere, world.

The lovingkindness meditation is a good model for us because, ultimately, it helps us enhance our capacity to envelop the whole world in lovingkindness by increasing our competence in replacing our automatic patterns with more mindful and thoughtful ones. One of the main reasons that I continue to chant is that the patterns of sound in my chant practice keep me mindful of my propensity to hear things in patterns and to stop myself when the pattern I see or hear is not the reality of the situation ("Stop! In the name of love …"). This is one of the hardest things for me, but I try to be mindful of how I as a body react to you as a body so that we can relate. This means it's essential that I know what's going on with/in me and why I react or respond the way I do. What makes me tick? What ticks me off? What buttons have been installed in me, what buttons have I installed on my own, and who knows how to push them? What are my propensities when trying to communicate with others? with God? What gets in the way of my living in my most compassionate place? And finally, what can I say or do to get to that place more of the time? Following is the most popular mantra in the world to help you get to that place.

Om Mani Padme Hum

> Every person whose heart is moved by love and compassion, who deeply and sincerely acts for the benefit of others without concern for fame, profit, social position, or recognition, expresses the activity of Chenrezig/Avalokiteshvara.
>
> —Bokar Rinpoche

This six-syllable mantra is called the Mani and is sometimes translated as "Hail to the jewel in the lotus." You may have seen a prayer wheel (mani wheel) being used. Most prayer wheels have a scroll on the inside filled with many repetitions of the mantra rolled around the spinning core. They also usually have the mantra written in a more ornate fashion on the outside. It is the mantra of Avalokiteshvara, the bodhisattva of compassion, the earthly form of the Buddha Amitabha. In Tibetan it is pronounced as Om Mani Peme Hung and is the mantra of Chenrezig—for our purpose they're essentially the same. Avalokiteshvara/Chenrezig was just about to enter nirvana when, instead of jumping over the wall to eternal bliss, he turned around and came back to help all the earthly beings get there, too. A real mensch. Om Mani Padme Hum is said to contain all 84,000 sections of the Buddha's teachings. It is essentially about increasing compassion by promoting spiritual growth and service to all.

Pronunciation Key and Definitions

Aum/Om Let yourself be absorbed by your generous
Buddha self at the deepest level in order to remove the
causes of suffering in our lives.

Ma (pronounced mah) means "jewel" or "diamond" and
represents an enlightened mind (your Buddha nature).
Picture it in the center of the flower that is your heart.

Ni (pronounced knee) brings patience.

Padme (pronounced pahd-meh) These two syllables mean
"lotus" and represent the potential of human consciousness. The lotus flower may have its roots in the mud at
the bottom of the pond, but what a beautiful flower!
Imagine your heart blossoming like that.

Hum (pronounce the *u* like "book") is a seed syllable that
brings wisdom and the way to achieve it.

Here's a version of the chant in Tibetan:

At this point I should probably say that if you want to use a mantra
for someone else, it is best to ask permission first, unless you're
doing it for your own children. There's a difference between
prayer and mantra. With prayer, God gets to decide the final result,
and with mantra you're deciding what's needed. Of course, if the
person is seriously ill, I feel it's okay to say a mantra on their behalf,
but the decision to undertake a discipline on someone's behalf usu-

ally comes out of my prayer life. It's not to be taken lightly, because you are messing around with other people's energy.

> The emergence and blossoming of understanding, love, and intelligence has nothing to do with any tradition—no matter how ancient or impressive—it has nothing to do with time. It happens completely on its own when a human being questions, wonders, listens, and looks without getting stuck in fear. When self-concern is quiet, in abeyance, heaven and earth are open.
>
> —Toni Packer

CHANTING FOR THE LIGHT

I mentioned earlier that I am not a morning person. This has caused me to look for things to make the morning bearable. I know that we live on a beautiful planet, but I tend not to care about that in the morning. I need something to remind me about wonder, serenity, flowers that blossom in the morning, and the warmth of the sun, preferably before I start rushing around to get to the next thing. There's a traditional Native American chant whose text is "The dawning of a new day is coming. Golden light is flowing all over the earth." The text is both literal and figurative in that the chant is used at the winter solstice to welcome the return of the light, and it also invokes our conscious awakening. If you want to find a great selection of chants for the elements, the four directions, earth and sky, and the animal, vegetable, and mineral kingdoms, as well as hundreds of other chants from all traditions, check out *Circle of Song* compiled by Kate Marks (see the resources list, p. 150). I would like, though, to share a couple of my morning chants in this section and the next.

ZUNI SUNRISE CALL

For the Ashiwi (Zuni) people, the sunrise is a sacred time. There's no distinction in their language between *daylight* and *life*. The Zuni Sunrise Call is a traditional chant for calling the sunrise. It is one of the most beautiful chants I know. The day just seems brighter when I sing this; I start out on an even keel, and the tune dictates a slow, steady tempo, which helps me to feel grounded.

Translation

Rise! Arise! Arise!
Wake ye, arise
Life is greeting thee
Ever watchful be
Mother Life-God
She is calling thee
Mother Life-God
She is greeting thee
Rise! Arise! Arise!

Zuni Sunrise Call

Let your mind be quiet, realizing the beauty of the world,
and the immense, the boundless treasures that it holds in store.
All that you have within you, all that your heart desires,

all that your nature so specially fits you for—
that or the counterpart of it waits
embedded in the great Whole, for you.
It will surely come to you.
Yet equally surely not one moment before its appointed time
will it come.
All your crying and fever and reaching out of hands
will make no difference.
Therefore do not begin that game at all.
Do not recklessly spill the waters of your mind
in this direction and in that,
lest you become like a spring lost and dissipated in the desert.
But draw them together into a little compass,
and hold them still, so still;
And let them become so clear—so limpid, so mirror-like;
At last the mountains and the sky shall glass themselves
in peaceful beauty,
And the antelope shall descend to drink, and to gaze
at his reflected image,
and the lion to quench his thirst,
And Love himself shall come and bend over,
and catch his own likeness in you.
—Edward Carpenter, "The Lake of Beauty"

The musical scale of holiness that we've been exploring is composed of pure energy. If we can understand what the different
types of energy are and how they work in us, how they work
on us, around us, and through us, we can learn how to give
ourselves little tune-ups. We can just let the awareness sink in
and not get in our way. This is as true when you're sitting
alone on your cushion as when you're in a group situation.

There are certain types of energy that we understand and like to play with. There are other types of energy that we just don't get, and still more energies that turn us off or leave us cold. The chants and mantras that we've explored so far are all about affecting the energy by changing the way our bodies vibrate. In his book *A Practical Guide to Vibrational Medicine,* Richard Gerber suggests that "on a subtle-energy level, some auto-immune disorders might be occurring in people who are (unconsciously) more self-critical than self-loving or accepting of themselves." Wait, there's more: "The wide spectrum of manifestations of heart-chakra dysfunction, from simple colds and respiratory infections to heart attacks and cancer, demonstrates how incredibly important the heart center is." So, love really does make the world go round. I know you know. Even the irksome people in our lives need love, deserve love, from us. It's hard to be enthusiastic and it can be a big task to find love to show, but look at it as life experience—what doesn't kill us makes us more loving. Besides, half the time the energy that drives me buggy about the irksome ones is the same energy that drives me buggy in myself. Ah, there's the rub. If we can't learn the lessons that love has to teach us as we pass through the different levels of our development, we have a harder time being happy.

Even though I've shared chants that will bring us enlightenment and transcendent knowledge, and even a couple that will help us not be reborn here again (the Ashtakshar mantra and the Rama Taraka mantra), those are not the most important aspects of the chants for me. Michelangelo, when he was eighty-seven, said, "I am still learning." That's what I'm aiming for, to learn as long as I live. Especially if it feels good. I don't care about rebirth, because I can only live in one world at a time. I'm looking forward to learning about the levels I most want to understand. At this point in my life, they are the levels I understand least. Light is the biggest mystery of all of them.

GAYATRI MANTRA

The sheer quantity of chants to honor and invoke the light—sun and moon, internally and externally—makes it almost impossible to whittle down the list to one or two to use in my practice. So I mostly rotate them. I even used Paul Robeson's version of "This Little Light of Mine" for a couple of years in the late eighties, for no reason except that I fell in love with it. When I auditioned for a big choir job but didn't want to sing an aria I didn't care about, I went in and sang the Robeson with my guitar. I knew that I could sing it and that they'd be able to find out everything they needed to know about my voice if they heard me sing it. Everyone told me I was nuts, and at the audition I got a look that made me think everyone was right, but I got the gig anyway. My point is that the chants you use don't have to be adored by everyone, or even be the fairest in the land. What's important is how they make you feel—the energy that they bring to your life.

The energy I most want to bring into my life is the energy of light. I've always wanted to be like the light (don't know why). Then I met Pat Moffitt Cook, who is one of those people who radiate light (she's a big smarty, too). She runs the Open Ear Center in Washington State, which is dedicated to sound and music in health and education. She's a provider of the Tomatis method (remember the monks in chapter 1?), and she teaches therapeutic applications of cross-cultural music in healing. She taught me the Gayatri mantra that I'm going to share with you. I've chanted it almost every day since then, and I'm always finding out new and cool things about it. This is a mantra for a lifetime, and if you choose it, you will be changed.

Gayatri generally means "song" or "hymn." It's also a literary meter in Sanskrit, composed of twenty-four syllables (three times eight). But its most important role is as the most sacred mantra of the Veda. The Gayatri is a hymn to the light, and the light shines everywhere. There are many symbolic explanations of the Gayatri, and one myth traditionally ascribes its genesis to the sage Vishvamitra, who has an interesting history of trying to attain spiritual power. He started out motivated by greed and envy, moved on to girl trouble, then pride, and so on, but every time he crashed and burned he went back and tried again. He was very persistent, and perseverance is the key. Lesson No. 16: As long as you stay plugged in, the juice will flow. The Gayatri is the result of his realizing that he would achieve his highest aspirations at the same time as he realized what a jerk he'd been. He was starting to do another *really* stupid thing (bash his head on a rock in remorse), when Vasistha (the most powerful Brahma-rishi) saved him from himself by sending a bolt of energy into him. The Gayatri mantra was his response to the transformation that resulted from the energy bolt.

There are many translations of the mantra, as well as many musical and mantra settings of the Gayatri. If you type *Gayatri Mantra* into your favorite computer search engine, you could spend hours sifting through the results. It was traditionally chanted at sunrise, noon, and sunset, and it was given by a guru to a student at sunrise, standing in a body of water while offering water to the sun. Even though Savitur (God symbolized as the sun) is male, and traditionally the Gayatri was given only to boys at their initiation (upanaya, the sacred thread ceremony), Gayatri is personified as a goddess, and I definitely feel a balance of male and female energy as I chant this mantra. The Gayatri is now considered a universal mantra, and everyone is encouraged to use it. It is said that chanting the Gayatri purifies the chanter, and listening to the Gayatri purifies the listener— that it is as good at ridding us of ignorance as the sun is at destroying darkness. The Gayatri is called the Mother of the Vedas, the creating light, the whole universe as it has come to be, and the Word that sings forth and protects the universe. The Gayatri is chanted to illumine the mind of our heart, not for personal gain. According to Raimundo Panikkar, the first mantra, which opens the whole Vedic revelation, is dedicated to Agni, the sacrificial fire "who transforms all human gifts into spiritual and divine realities so that they may reach their endless destination." Agni is made up of three inseparable aspects: divine, human, and earthly. Panikkar goes on to say that we invoke the Divine because "filled with love, we sense within ourselves a gulf between the finite and the infinite, and simply open the sluices that enclose our finitude." This is the context into which the Gayatri was born. It follows as the very next mantra.

There are two forms of the Gayatri mantra, the long form and the short form. I was taught the long form first, and that's what I use, but most people use the short form. The difference is that the long form uses all of the chakras, while the short form only uses the first three. I have never heard of a reason for doing one rather than the other. So if you'd like to use the short form, just remove the second line. Each of the last three lines illuminates an aspect of light: the ultimate internal radiance of the divine life-giver, symbolized by Savitur, the sun; the brilliance of the living god who illumines everything; and the light in us. Here is how it is translated in Panikkar's *The Vedic Experience:* "We meditate upon the glorious splendor of the Vivifier Divine. May he himself illumine our minds."

There are so many translations of this mantra that I've cobbled together the meanings that speak to me.

Pronunciation Key and Definitions

Om in this case means "God."

Bhur (pronounced boor) means "vital energy" *(prana),* and is associated with the root chakra.

Bhuvaha (pronounced boo-vah-hah) is for the polarity chakra.

Swaha (pronounced swah-hah) is for the solar plexus chakra.

Maha (pronounced mah-hah) is for the heart chakra.
Janaha (pronounced jah-nah-hah) is for the throat chakra.
Tapaha (pronounced tah-pah-hah) is for the third eye
   chakra.
Satyam (pronounced sutt-yum) is for the crown chakra.
Tat (pronounced taht) means "that," representing ultimate
   reality—God.
Savitur (pronounced sah-vee-toor) means "Divine Sun,
   Creator, and Preserver."
Varenyam (pronounced vahr-en-yum) means "supreme."
Bhargo (pronounced bhahr-go) means "destroyer of sins."
Devasya (pronounced deh-vahs-yah) means "divine grace."
Dhimahi (pronounced dee-mah-hee) means "may we
   receive."
Dhiyo (pronounced dhee-yo) means "intellect."
Yo (pronounced yo) means "who."
Naha (pronounced na-ha) means "our."
Prachodayat (pronounced prah-cho-die-yaht) means "may
   inspire."

Om Bhur, Om Buvaha, Om Swaha

Om Maha, Om Janaha, Om Tapaha, Om Satyam

Om Tat Savitur Varenyam

Bhargo Devasya Dhimahi

Dhiyo Yonaha Prachodayat

AHAM PREMA

For most of us, our intention is to try to create love and live a
happy life while we're here. Bad stuff will undoubtedly happen,
but if we can center ourselves and manifest lovingkindness and

compassion within, our task will be much easier because we will be able to distill the spiritual reality that is God to its essence. Panikkar says it will happen when outer reality, inner reality, and we ourselves coincide. That's what the Gayatri can help us do. Nurturing love, kindness, and compassion are The Big Deal. But it is still sometimes difficult for us to see the coincidence of the three. The question arises: How can I possibly be an image of God for someone else if I can't find God in myself?

When we take the time to reflect on our lives as an image of the divine presence, we make more light. We become the light. Chants are like icons (from the Greek *eikon,* meaning "likeness, image") in the sense that they give us ways to express the divine presence. They may be pretty to look at, but they're not decorations. Their physical aspects are not important. Their purpose is to teach us to embody the spiritual qualities of the light.

Aham prema can be translated as "I am divine love." When I use this chant, I find myself beginning with my full voice (to get it through my thick skull?), but I notice after a while that I'm much calmer, and that my voice is a barely audible whisper. The power of Aham Prema lies in its ability to take away your doubts and defenses and let you rest in nurturing love, light, kindness, and compassion. That is what you are. This is a mantra that we can hold in our hearts all the way through life's lessons. As you say Aham Prema, try to accept that you are divine love; hold it in your cupped hands, hold the Divine in your hands; hold it in your heart, hold the divine love that's already in your heart. There is no place for anything but aham prema. You are divine love ... aham prema. Say to yourself, "I am divine love." Try to grasp that. Try to accept it. Know that you are divine love, just as you are.

Pronunciation Key and Definitions

Aham (pronounced ah-hahm) means "I."
Prema (pronounced preh-mah) means "love, divine love."

Try it with me: aham prema, aham prema.

Tag, you're it.

CHAPTER SEVEN

NOW THAT YOU'RE CHANTING: NUTS AND BOLTS

In this chapter we'll look at some ways to approach your new practice. I'll share some things that I've found helpful, a couple of ideas to play with, and a few phrases for reflection that have been meaningful for me and may also be meaningful for you.

Things will crop up for you when you're chanting that seemingly have nothing to do with chanting, yet nevertheless there they are. Try to pay attention to them as they surface, and then just let them go. These things often mean something—not always, but when they're different from the usual suspects, take note and see if they crop up again. Often it takes a while for their meaning to become clear, and then it takes a while longer for you to discern what (if anything) to do about them. I see this as a practical application of the "spirit blowing where it will." My job is to watch it blow, sometimes to blow along with it, sometimes to listen to the sound of its blowing, sometimes to just follow it— through the trees, past my ears as I sit next to the river, or over the hill in front of my house, past the beehive flag on our front porch, looking for all the world like something I've never seen, or something that I just can't place. The meaning isn't the point. The point is in being reflectively mindful, in paying attention to what is actually going on, both with me, and with not-me. This requires courage and patience. It requires living in the actuality of now, and not in the fear-filled place of what if. It's hard to live right here now, because there's always a to-do list. The list can wait.

In the bookstore where I work, the biggest-selling books are in the spirituality section. From what I see, people have a vague hope and trust that things will work out, and almost everyone says they're spiritual. But although spirit may be the animating principle in our lives, it's not really the driving force. Our cultural spirituality looks like a very broad, very shallow pool that can dry up at the first spell of discomfort. I think we're more culturally driven than we'd like to admit, and we're mostly driven by desire and a fear of failure. As a society, we're bombarded every day by images of things we may or may not need or want. They come at us so quickly and furiously that we don't have the time to take them in (like an ad going by on the side of a bus), or we choose not to discern whether we do in fact truly desire whatever is being peddled. It's time to focus our power of choice on our humanity, and to place our experience at the heart of the matter. Think of your practice as an aid to societal wellness. The task is to figure out how to remain engaged while still maintaining a certain healthy distance, so we're not deafened by the roar of the crowd, depressed by the stories we read in the newspapers and see on television, or constantly distressed by the events of our lives. The decision we must make first is which voices will we allow to have power over our thoughts. Managing this energy takes practice. Edward Carpenter, an early twentieth-century poet, philosopher, and mystic, puts it this way:

> Obtain power over your thoughts and you are free. If you
> want to obtain that priceless power of commanding

thought—of using or dismissing it (for the two things go together) at will—there is no way but practice. And the practice consists in two exercises: *(a)* that of concentration—in holding the thought steadily for a time on one subject, or point of a subject; and *(b)* that of effacement—in effacing any given thought from the mind and determining not to entertain it for such and such a time. Both these exercises are difficult. Failure in practicing them is certain—and may extend over years. But the power equally certainly grows with practice. And ultimately there may come a time when the learner is not only able to efface from his mind any given thought (however importunate), but may even succeed in effacing, during short periods, all thought of any kind. When this stage is reached the veil of illusion which surrounds all mortal things is pierced and the entrance to the Paradise of Rest (and of universal power and knowledge) is found.

Chanting will help you to build commanding power over your thoughts. Like Carpenter said, failure is certain over the years, but the power does grow with practice. The extended periods of silence after a chant are the place where thought is effaced. The process set in motion by consciously directing the energy of your thoughts is the beginning of wisdom, and of knowing that you are the energy that links you to the rest of the cosmos. This is where creativity begins. In the same way that seeking peace in the world requires us to first manifest that peace in ourselves, becoming truly mindful in composing our internal decisions ultimately will make it easier for us to creatively hear where we as a civilization are to go next. Chanting helps us to honor the wisdom and knowing of that creative process as it is given to us, and as we discern its steps.

I'd like to share a set of directions for singing that I've found very helpful, and to which I often refer. Everything on this list is important to bear in mind. It was originally published as "Directions for Singing" by Charles Wesley in his 1761 collection *Select Hymns*. Wesley was an Englishman who composed more than six thousand hymns in his lifetime. I found it on a bulletin board in a choir room long ago, and have adapted the language to be a little more modern. I've tried to be faithful to the spirit of the original.

Directions for Chanting

1. Learn each chant thoroughly; take it to heart. Learn as many as you please this way.
2. Listen closely and try to sing the chants as they are taught, without altering or mending them at all.
3. Sing often with others, as frequently as you can. Don't decide to pass up a chance to chant with others because you're tired or stressed out. Go anyway, sing with your whole soul, and you will find it a blessing. Trust me.
4. Chant with your whole body, and with good courage. Be careful not to chant as if you are half-asleep; lift up your voice with strength. Don't fear the sound of your voice, and do not be ashamed of its being heard by others. Aim for a unity of spirit. Your voice is a unique gift from God, given for your health and happiness.
5. Sing modestly. Don't bawl, or try to drown out your neighbor who doesn't sing as well as you, so you can be heard above and distinct from the rest of the group. Chant with the intent of making harmony, and strive to unite your voice together with other voices to make one clear, melodious sound.
6. Sing in time. Make an effort to identify and stay with the group pulse. Listen to the leading voices and breathe with them so you don't fall behind the group beat. This will help to entrain the group energy, and build a sound community.

7. Above all, sing spiritually. Have an ear to God in every word you sing. Aim at hearing God more than pleasing yourself or anyone else. In order to do this, attend to the sense of what you sing, and see that you don't get carried away with the sound, but offer your song to God and the group continually.

By now you probably have some idea of what you'd like to work on, or at least have a chant that's beginning to stick. To start, try a couple of chants on for size. Sing through a number of different chants multiple times, maybe twelve, eighteen, or twenty-seven repetitions each. Think of it as an exercise in discernment. Here's what I do:

Set an intention, whether you're chanting to stop a war, to heal the pain of loss, to focus on a specific aspect of your energy, or for someone you love.

Write it on a piece of paper.

On another sheet of paper, make a list of possible chants that might effect change on your situation (see the index of chants, p. 159).

Fold the paper with your intention and put it away in a safe place for the duration of the discipline.

Hum for a minute or two to center yourself.

Try the first chant on your list twelve times and see what comes up. The most important time to listen is when you finish chanting each one. You may sit in silence for a minute or two (or five).

Pay attention to the quality of the silence. How do you feel? How's your posture? What's up? If a chant seems to want to continue, keep it in the running

(sometimes I'll just let them go until they stop). If
one seems to want to stop sooner, try it again next
time.
Move to the next chant on your list. Sing through as many
as you like, and whittle it down to one or two or three.
You've already begun!

I generally undertake forty-day disciplines. I'll pick one or
two short mantras or chants and do them in the morning, five
days a week, 108 times a day. I also have one or two long chants
for which I do fewer repetitions, both morning and evening.
When it's time to begin a new cycle I sing through the bija
mantra, and any other chants that I'm drawn to or that come up,
and try to hear where to go next. Alternately, I open a book and
see what's there. The serendipitous approach is in knowing that
what you need will be provided for you. Sometimes I have to look
further than the page I open to, but sometimes what I'm looking
for is right there waiting for me, even if I wasn't sure what I was
looking for when I picked up the book in the first place.

Set a time and a place to chant, preferably the same time and
place every day (it's getting to be a habit with me). If you choose
to chant twice a day, two different places are fine. Traditionally,
the most powerful times to chant are during the two hours
before sunrise and during the two hours before sunset. Think of
these hours as liminal space, as God's time, the kind of threshold
that community grows out of. There is an aspect of transformation that happens in these hours that enables us to stand between
our everyday world and a real encounter with the Holy One.
The Celts call these times "thin places."

Always ask for what you want or need, knowing you may
or may not get it. But have faith that what you *will* always be
given is the spirit of God, a creative way to tackle whatever it is
that needs tackling, and a whole lotta light. Don't forget the
incredible beauty of the light. You are in its keeping.

Many people practice when they wake up and before they go to bed. That doesn't work for me because I need coffee in the morning, and when my head hits the pillow, it's a minute or two of hara breathing and the next thing I know it's morning again! However, the first time I did a Hanuman (the monkey-faced god) mantra, Hanuman visited me in my dreams and woke me up, and the mantra would not stop. What a rotten night of sleep that was, compounded by a strange and uncomfortable bed. I'd *never* been moved by Hanuman before, and his manner of arrival didn't incline me to invite him right in. At that time I had been singing the traditional Kuan Yin mantra for well over a year almost exclusively, and I felt like I was just starting to get it. I was chanting at a group weekend, so I checked out every possible reason Hanuman had bugged me all night. I asked around the group, and a couple of people had noticed that his presence was strong, but they hadn't lost sleep over it. Turned out Hanuman was bugging me because it was time to attend to some issues that had been messing with my self-esteem and my voice, in the sense of finding it and using it. Oh, is that all?

Om Hum Hanumate Vijayam is now permanently installed in my body. *Hum* is the seed sound for the throat chakra. Hum is like its own little invocation and feels very healing. The Dalai Lama says that Hum represents the unity of wisdom and method. It's seated in the throat chakra, and eliminates illness and obstructions there. It's also good for learning languages.

ABOUT RULES AND PRACTICES

I tend to make sound everywhere I go, much to the consternation of many people (especially those called to the contemplative life). I'm often tapped on the shoulder while riding the train (by my partner, Susan), to alert me to the fact that I'm singing out loud. You'd think I'd notice when the sound was going "out there" and when it was staying "in here," but I'm afraid the reality is that all boundaries are permeable. I find this idea oddly comforting; maybe I'm not as dense as I think I am. I've always wondered if there was a "proper way to chant," but I never bothered worrying about it too much beyond the directions for singing. One reason I haven't bothered is that I'm not big on rules, and I have seen huge lists of rules that, if broken, will get you sent right into the fiery furnace. There are zealots in every faith who want things to be done the right and proper way. But this is chanting—how dangerous can it be? You're opening your mouth and making sound that will enhance your spiritual life. I think that if you chant with faith and an open heart, even if you mispronounce a word or two inadvertently, God will be okay with it. Some of God's followers may not, but many a fine religious path has been spoiled for people by the treatment they've received at the hands of the followers of that path. That is not to say that you shouldn't try to learn the right way to do things, if you can figure it out. But I went online one day, looking for the correct pronunciation of a mantra, and I found four different pronunciations, each purporting to be the only right and proper one. Should I wait until I find conclusive information before using the mantra, or should I give it my best shot and trust that the information will show up when I need it?

There's a story told about the mantra Om Mani Padme Hum, in which a young scholar had the opportunity to travel by boat to visit with an old hermit, who was highly regarded. The scholar was excited because they shared the same mantra. When the young man arrived, he was horrified to hear the old man pronouncing the mantra incorrectly. He was glad he came, because otherwise the hermit could have spent the rest of his life saying it wrong. The hermit, a humble man, was very grateful to learn the correct pronunciation. The scholar left, feeling that he'd done his good deed by instructing the old man, and got on the boat to go home. Soon after, he saw the boatman looking dumbfounded. The young man turned to see the hermit standing next to the boat. The old man said, "Excuse me, but I've forgotten the correct pronunciation. Can you please tell me again?" The young man mumbled something like "You obviously don't need it," but the hermit politely asked until the scholar yielded and gave him the answer he sought. The hermit was heard repeating the mantra, mindfully, over and over, as he walked back to the shore across the water's surface.

Another reason I don't worry too much about the rules is that I don't count very well. When I'm singing, I can barely count to three without losing my place. I use a bead mala (a rosary—mine has 108 beads) to help me, but then I find myself forgetting to move my fingers to the next bead. I sometimes wonder how on God's green earth people can count to 108 and still pay attention to the chants, let alone count to 125,000, the number of repetitions some disciplines require. Even 10,000 repetitions sound like a lot, I know, but it's not as hard as you think for a mantra to have its transformative way with you. I went to my calculator to figure it out: It's only 92⅔ days if you chant 108 repetitions every day. If you chant 108 times morning and evening, you can make it to 10,000 repetitions in 46⅓ days. That's about six weeks and should be fairly manageable. If you are one of those people who can compartmentalize in that way, and keep count and listen and focus, and all the things that trip me up, then go with God. If, however, you are like me and keep losing count every other minute, I'd like to suggest the time method.

After you've figured out which chant or mantra you'll be using, look at the clock, note the time, start your engine, and begin chanting. Try your best to keep track of the count, and do 108 repetitions. When you finish, look at the clock to see how long it took. That's how long it takes, give or take a couple of repetitions. You may get faster if you don't have to count, but don't shorten the time, because you may also be slower some days. Be thankful for one less thing to think about (during the time you're not supposed to be thinking about things), and trust that it will all work out in your chakras; the energy will be sent to the right place. Have I mentioned the reason for 108 repetitions? It's because the Vedas teach that there are 108 astral channels that lead from your heart to the rest of your subtle body. Or because there are 108 names for Ganesh, Krishna, Shiva, and many other gods, including the Holy One.

I've found it very helpful, when first starting out, to chant only parts of mantras or prayers, and even single words. Aum/Om by itself can keep you occupied for months. I still do it when I'm trying to choose a new mantra, and sometimes I'm just drawn to a part of a chant or mantra. "Om a hung" (the beginning of the Padmasambhava mantra) is a very powerful purification practice (see the audio resources list, p. 157). "Be still and know that I am God" is also an excellent stress reducer. Flip through the book and make a list of the words or phrases that move you. Experiment with them, chanting them on one note for forty days. You'll be surprised at what might happen. I was.

Other ways to practice include experimenting with the standard forms from your own faith tradition and plugging in chants. There's a beautiful guide for a Shabbat morning service by Rabbi Goldie Milgram on the Reclaiming Judaism Web site. Here's an evening ritual I often sing mostly on one note. I've loosely adapted it from the Order for Compline in the Book of Common Prayer (from the Episcopal Church):

> Aum/Om
> God grant us a peaceful night and a beautiful end. Amen.
> Our help is in the name of the Holy One; The maker of
>   heaven and earth, and of us all.
> *Silence*
> May God grant us the grace and comfort of the Holy
>   Spirit. Amen.
> O God, make speed to save us. O God, make haste to
>   help us.

Glory to the Holy One of Spirit: as it was in the beginning, is now, and will be forever. Amen.

Sing a psalm or chant

Glory to the Holy One of Spirit: as it was in the beginning, is now, and will be forever. Amen.

Read a passage of Scripture (a traditional suggestion follows)

> God has not given us a spirit of fear, but of power, and of love, and of a sound mind. (2 Timothy 1:7)

Give thanks

Sing a chant

Say some prayers (here are a couple of classics; feel free to use your own)

> Into your hands I commend my spirit; For you have redeemed me, O God of truth.
>
> Keep me as the apple of your eye; Hide me under the shadow of your wings.

> Holy One, our only Home, hallowed be your Name.
> May your day dawn, your will be done here, as in heaven.
> Feed us today, and forgive us as we forgive each other.
> Do not forsake us at the test, but deliver us from evil.
> For the glory, the power, and the mercy are yours, now and forever. Amen.

> Keep watch, dear Lord, with those who work, or watch, or weep this night, and give your angels charge over those who sleep. Tend the sick, Lord Christ; give rest to the weary, bless the dying, soothe the suffering, pity the afflicted, shield the joyous; and all for your love's sake. Amen.

Hear our prayers; and let our cry come to you.
Silence
Guide us waking, and guard us sleeping; that awake we
   may walk in love, and asleep we may rest in peace.
Offer blessings and give thanks
Sing a chant
Aum/Om/Amen

CREATIVE OPTIONS

There are so many options available that you should have no trouble at all finding ways to use chant in your prayer life. Be creative! Start a chant/prayer journal, and fill it with beautiful prayers, quotes, stories, and chants. Then use it. It will make you happy.

Some ways to organize your journal include the following:

Organizing by time: Time of day—morning, noon,
   evening, bedtime (see chapter 4 for the traditional
   Benedictine hours); days of the week; weeks of the
   month; months of the year.
Organizing by type of petition: Wisdom; light; love; healing;
   peace; pain; earth; compassion; intuition; trust; justice;
   joy; praying for others; praying for yourself; blessings;
   thanksgivings; and so on.

Here's an idea for a ritual based on my morning practice, if you want to start out by following a path already well trod. At any time feel free to venture off into a pretty thicket.

Opening prayer (1–2 minutes)
Silence (2–20 minutes)
Humming with a set intention (3–5 minutes)
Chakra bija mantra (5 minutes)
Gayatri mantra (9 or 36 or 108 times)
Kuan Yin mantra (9 times)

USING INSTRUMENTS, OR HOW I FELL IN LOVE WITH A SINGING BOWL

There is something very challenging yet satisfying about sitting with one or two notes at a time and finding your place in relationship to them. I have spent at least two years of my life totally engaged with C-sharp and G-sharp. Being in relationship with a couple of notes isn't as odd as you might think. There is a quality about those particular notes that reached right inside of me and touched me deeply. They say that each of us has our own note, one that moves us in a way no other note does.

I was unpacking a box at the bookstore where I work, and there were a few singing bowls in the order. As I unwrapped each one, I struck it gently with a beater to check for cracks and to make sure it had a nice clear sound. Each bowl has its own particular notes and overtones that are unique to it. In his book *The Mysticism of Sound and Music,* Hazrat Inayat Khan says that everything in the world speaks to us, and the more our inner senses are open to listening, the more will be revealed, and consequently, the more we will be able to understand. This was certainly the case that day in the store. I unwrapped the biggest bowl last, because the others had been stacked inside it. It was a lot heavier than the others, weighing about five pounds. When I first heard the sound of that bowl, the effect was immediate. It resonated in me in a way that no other bowl before or since has, and I knew that we were meant for each other. Its fundamental tone is a C-sharp (said to be the note of creation), its secondary tone is a G-sharp, and its tertiary note an E an octave higher, making a C-sharp minor chord. I'd never heard anything like it.

For weeks after bringing the bowl home, I would hold the bowl and rub a stick around its rim until my arm hurt. I wouldn't realize my arm hurt until I was finished, but if you try holding a five-pound bag of sugar in front of you with your elbow braced on your thigh, for an hour or two, you'll get the picture. My goal was twofold: first, to figure out why these particular notes had such an effect on me, which led to my getting acquainted with the chakras (Getting to know me, getting to know all about me …). The other, more "practical" goal was to be able to move the stick effortlessly (Hah! Anything you do takes effort—Lesson No. 11,463) around the edge of the bowl while avoiding the distracting sound it made when the stick bounced off the side of the bowl. This is what would happen when I lost my focus. I found that it was possible to change from the C-sharp to the G-sharp, as well as to play them both at the same time. However, it took months to be able to move between the notes before I could bring them in and out smoothly. After a while, I began to hum with the bowl. Long tones, for long periods of time. The power of a continuous tone felt like home, and I was happy to dwell there. Slowly, I began to add tones and sing simple chants and songs with the bowl as accompaniment. About two years later, original chants began to come in. I say "come in" because it was like a channel had been changed in my body, and all of a sudden I wrote chants, whereas I had only written tunes before. It was like I'd tuned in to a new radio station that I owned shares in. That's about the time I went to the beach during hurricane season with the beautiful book of blessings.

Ten years later I can appreciate how these exercises were vital to my development (musically and otherwise), and I highly recommend them. By listening deeply to the drone of the bowl for an extended period, then gradually joining my voice with it, I was able to expand my comfort level with various intervals and dissonances (both internally and externally). Chants began to spontaneously appear as I was reading poetry, I think because I was listening as I was reading. There's a connectedness that occurred when I was reading that I don't recall being there before. It was as if I literally heard and felt the vibrations as I read. I know this is the reality, but all of a sudden it went to my core *and* was very conscious and up-front. This led to an improvement in my skill at reading aloud. One of the great delights at our house is reading a good book out loud. I am the designated reader because my partner does handwork (knitting, counted cross stitch, etc.), and because it brings us a shared joy. My time with the singing bowl also brought me a sense of security as an improviser, a skill that I did not possess at all before I spent so much time playing with one note. It also made me better at multitasking—and smarter about knowing when not to do it.

I often use the singing bowl in worship services so I can keep a smooth sound going while people pray. It's like casting a circle of sound, which envelops the group and helps them focus on the prayers. The bowl transports people powerfully (like magic) to the inner realm, in a way that almost everyone notices immediately. I once met a Supreme Court justice because he came up to me after a worship service. He said, "I need to know what was making that sound." Many people need to know the same thing every time I ring it.

With a little digging, I found out that Tibetan singing bowls were traditionally made from the seven precious metals. Each metal is associated with a celestial body: gold for the sun, silver for the moon, mercury for Mercury, copper for Venus, iron for Mars, tin for Jupiter, and lead for Saturn. Since these are the "precious" metals, you'll never be sure that every bowl contains each metal, and it's commonly thought that not every metal is actually present in every bowl. Unfortunately, since China invaded Tibet in 1949, many monasteries have been destroyed, so there hasn't been much of a need for new bowls. There are some new ones being made in Nepal, although they're usually made mostly of brass and copper. You can spot the newer ones by their shine. If you think you'd like to purchase a bowl, I recommend doing this in person, rather than on the Internet. Listen for clear ringing tone—it should make you feel a sense of focus or clarity that "speaks to you." You're looking for something that just "takes you there."

As for the care and feeding of bowls, they don't need much. I never clean or polish mine, even though some people think it would look nicer if I did. It's old, and I suppose I just like old dirt. I'd hate to remove the signs of the previous "owner." There are many other instruments that can enhance your practice in one way or another. Something with a sustained sound (a drone) is nice so you can concentrate on your own sound, not the drone's sound, but almost any instrument will work (except maybe a kazoo).

BECOMING A BEAD-COUNTER

The word *bead* comes from the Anglo Saxon verb "bid," as in "to pray." Carl Jung had a sign carved over his front door and on his tombstone that said, "Bidden or not, God is present." I'll try to run you barefoot through the beads, limiting myself to the really important stuff, because I find them to be a helpful organizer. More than that, though, your own mala or rosary will become infused with your spirit and the spirit of your prayers. Mine reminds me of the integration that I strive for through the use of sacred speech.

Throughout history, strings of beads have been used for many purposes. Hindu malas contain 108 beads plus a bead called the meru or guru bead. The meru is where the energy is built up by the constant repetition. When you finish the 108 repetitions of your chosen chant, you turn the mala around and go back the way you came for the next 108 repetitions. I was taught that you never go across the meru bead—that's like going against your teacher. Buddhist malas developed from the Hindu practice as a way to enhance goodness while clearing the system of the 108 toxins. Traditionally, 108 also represents the number of sinful desires we have to overcome before we reach enlightenment. So much for that.

The Iroquois nation used strings of shells and beads (what Europeans called wampum) as a kind of record-keeper for their history. Each bead represented a community event. The Sikhs use 108 knots of wool. There are cultures in China and South America that use knotted ropes in lengths of 108 knots, and other cultures use pebbles. What is important is how the unity of body and mind is made possible by the use of your beads with intention. They will become a record-keeper as they become infused with the spirit of your practice.

Although Roman Catholic laypeople had earlier used a string of beads to pray the 150 psalms or repeat the Lord's Prayer, the traditional Catholic rosary (*rosarium* means "rose garden") is said to have originated as an antidote to heretical practices in Toulouse, France, during the time of the Albigensian sect in the twelfth and thirteenth centuries. Saint Dominic preached against the Cathari (or "pure ones") and taught that meditation on what Jesus and his mother Mary had done for us was preferable to their practices. What has developed from the repetition of fifteen decades (sets of ten beads) of the Hail Mary with a Lord's Prayer before and a Gloria Patri after for each of the series of holy mysteries (joyful, sorrowful, and glorious mysteries, and the recently added luminous mysteries) is an amazing devotion to Mary the mother of Jesus, an appreciation among Catholics for the importance of the repetitive invoking of the Holy Name, and recognition of the efficacy of individual prayer in a clerical culture. In his book *The Invocation of the Name of Jesus,* Rama Coomaraswamy says that individual prayer "has the virtue of reestablishing equilibrium and restoring peace, in a word, opening us up to grace." That's why we do it. It is a way of developing the kingdom of God within us, which brings us closer together.

Islamic malas are called *masbaha* or *subha,* from *Subhan'u'llah,* which means "God is the all-splendorous." They usually contain ninety-nine beads, one for each of the names of God that we know, and they are divided in three sections, for the repetition of the following: *Subhan'u'llah; Alhamd'u'llah* ("Praise God"); and *Allah'u'Akbar* ("God is the most great"). They are also used for personal prayer.

Let me tell you right now that you don't need beads at all. I use them because they keep me mindful. I like to wear them on my wrist, and their presence reminds me to chant. I see the beads and think, "Hey, look, I chant." Invariably, a chant comes right in, and I start to chant.

What kind of rosary beads or malas will withstand daily use, and how do you take care of them? Are there any rules? I use a string of rosewood beads because they cost under twenty dollars and were knotted. I've found that having individual knots between the beads is a really good idea. Of course, I learned this the hard way. Last summer, on a plane to Memphis, I was sitting in a window seat, softly chanting at 29,000 feet, when all of a sudden I heard the sound of seeds on plastic: tap, tap, tap, roll, roll tap … I looked down and watched the seeds of the Tree of Enlightenment rolling along the floor toward first class. "Hmm," I thought. "A sign?" Lesson No. 17: Buy beads with a knot between each bead if you're going to use them every day. If you can't find any, buy what you like and restring them as soon as possible, so you don't lose so many at once. I recovered what I could and made them into smaller wrist malas because it seemed a shame to waste them. The saddest part of having my mala break on the airplane was that my beads were previously owned when I bought them, and I knew that I'd lost some of their history, and I could never recover that part of the record. My old beads also had two smaller counters (ten small beads on them inserted at the twenty-one-bead point on the larger mala), which I dutifully removed and tried to reuse. I put one on my new mala for a while, which I used to count the longer chants with fewer repetitions, but I kept getting it caught on things. Doors were very popular; at least every other day I'd get snagged on one. The night I got them stuck in the CD-ROM drive of my computer was the last straw; I'm obviously not responsible enough, nor can I pay enough attention to warrant keeping an extra counter on my beads. Nowadays, I just try to count to nine on my own. Sometimes I almost make it, but mostly I lose it around four, five, six, seven. So, I do extras to appease the gods.

Almost any material will work for beads, and you should use the beads you are drawn to. Wood, seeds, stones, crystals, rose petals (rolled into beads—they smell great). Each material has a different quality: sandalwood and rudraksha beads are popular and powerful. Sandalwood is very aromatic and brings calm and focus. *Rudra* is one of the names of Shiva, and *aksha* means "tear." The rudraksha tree is said to originate from the tears of Lord Shiva and is good for focus and holding the energy of Shiva and Durga. Clear quartz crystal is good for clarity, to promote healing, and for relieving headaches and stress; hematite for protection; amethyst for wisdom; aventurine for growth of the heart; black onyx for self-mastery; blue-lace agate for psychic inspiration; carnelian for courage; garnet for transmuting energy; frosted crystal for peace. I won't go further into the different materials that have an effect on physical ailments (for example, amber for menstrual problems), but there's a wealth of information to be found in your local bookstore and on Web sites. You might like to string your own beads, which can be a very prayerful experience. Many of the people who string beads for a living pray their way through the day, infusing your beads with their prayers for you.

It's okay to wash your beads. I do it at the beginning of a chanting cycle, or if I drop them on the floor, or if I get paint on them (don't ask). There are a few rules I've read, some of which I follow and some of which I don't. Pretty much everyone agrees that you should hold the beads in your right hand. This is because traditionally the right is the side of offering, while the left is the side of receiving. Hold the mala or rosary between your thumb and middle finger, and rotate it around without using your index finger, which is said to have negative energy. You're not supposed to show your beads at all in some traditions, but it's okay to wear them in others. They shouldn't be held below the navel, but close to your heart. That one's hard for me because I often use mine on the train, and I hide them in my lap so I don't look like I'm the girl in sackcloth and ashes, all holier than thou.

If you choose to use beads, it's good to begin with a short prayer (something like "May the words of my mouth and the meditations of my heart always be acceptable in your sight"). Focus your attention on either your third eye chakra or your heart. Then visualize God within, sending all good through you and radiating all good out from you.

PHRASES FOR REFLECTION

In addition to the chants and mantras and individual words we've seen so far, here are some other phrases that I've collected and found helpful over the years. Use them, chant them, and add your own.

> Open my heart.
> May I live in harmony.
> The breath of all life blesses us.
> May I reflect a healing spirit.
> I trust this path will bring me joy.
> Let your light illumine me.
> May I become my sweetest self.
> Lead me to a balanced life.
> Guide us, guard us.
> Fill us with your spirit.
> May I find peace within.
> Help me free myself from doubt.
> Baruch atah Adonai Eloheynu melech ha olam asher kidzshanu (Hebrew for "Blessed is God, which makes us holy").
> Show me thy ways, teach me thy paths, and lead me in thy truth.

May I be more compassionate.
God is love is God.
May I begin and end in love.

GROWTH AND LISTENING

I'd like to share one last story. It's about a woman, a medieval abbess, composer, physician, and writer named Hildegard of Bingen (1098–1179). She was her mother's tenth child. At that time, the tenth child in an aristocratic family was considered the tithe child, so off she went to a convent at the age of eight. All her life she would tell people that she was uneducated, because she wasn't drilled in the method of rote learning and repetition that was commonly used. She was by nature a humble girl and saw herself as a feather on the breath of God.

Hildegard had visions from the time she was three, but she didn't tell anyone except her tutor about them until much later. At fifteen, Hildegard took her vows, and she lived an active Benedictine life. She prayed with people, and worked with people, and was steeped in the daily offices. Her room was next to the monastery chapel. As she grew up, she learned about the healing properties of herbs and flowers, the four elements, the four seasons, the four humors of the body, the four zones of the earth, and the four winds. Later she wrote about how they related to each other and the powers they possessed. She located the elements in the human body and wrote of balance, and how disease was caused by imbalance. She wrote about the sun and the moon and their effect on our health. She was the first nun to write about medicine, and her books, highly regarded at the time, are still in print. Throughout her life she had visions and felt a mounting pressure to speak out. She kept silent out of humility, and because her spiritual directors told her it wasn't her place to speak out—that she should just attend to the daily life of the convent (of which she was now the abbess).

In fact, Hildegard did not begin writing until her forty-third year, when she received a confirming vision and experienced a spiritual awakening. She wrote a letter to Bernard of Clairvaux for support, but his response was lukewarm. However, someone forwarded her letter to Pope Eugenius III, who was enthusiastic and gave her permission to continue. Hildegard was hesitant and afraid of speaking about things she'd kept silent about for so long. She said that she blushed at the thought. But she did speak out. She became a figure of authority in the second half of her life, speaking out against the Crusades and the general corruption in the church and in the world. She was often approached for her advice and counsel. She wrote many chants that are still sung today, and she strove to be faithful to what God was showing her. Words as well as music often accompanied her visions. The texts aren't linear—they don't tell a story but are more like images piled high, wholly intuited and circular, full of greenness, wisdom, spirit, fire, and abundant heart. She *knew* that God was pervasive.

Hildegard's chants were written for the liturgies of the church, mostly for the daily offices. They were plainsong in a florid style, usually based on biblical themes. However, she used the music to paint a picture of the words and sometimes even changed modes in the middle of a chant, something that hadn't been done before. This makes them seem almost improvised. They are some of the most difficult chants I've ever sung, but you'd never know it just by listening, because they're so meditative. A concept of harmony pervaded her entire life, and her chant seems like it is always in the process of becoming, partly because of the changing modes, which often don't resolve as we expect them to, and partly because the feel is so completely holistic. Hildegard's way of looking at the world was through a kind of prism of connected knowing. Music, medicine, spirituality, psychology, and all the stuff of life evolves in relation to everything else. Her way of knowing was clearly not the way favored in her time, and it is not the favored way in our time either. Nevertheless, Hildegard is a reminder that we, too, need to be faithful to what God is showing us and how, and that with conscious periods of quiet growth and listening, we'll know right where we are and be able to find our way together.

RESOURCES

BOOKS

HEALTH
Beinfield, Harriet, and Efrem Korngold. *Between Heaven and Earth: A Guide to Chinese Medicine.* New York: Ballantine Books, 1991.

Friedman, Robert L. *The Healing Power of the Drum.* Reno, Nev.: White Cliffs Media, 2000. The use of rhythm in the treatment of ADD, autism, Alzheimer's, and more.

Gerber, Richard. *A Practical Guide to Vibrational Medicine: Energy Healing and Spiritual Transformation.* New York: Quill, 2001. Contains an eye-opening discussion of the chakras and their energy from a medical doctor.

Moffitt Cook, Pat. *Shaman, Jhankri and Néle: Music Healers of Indigenous Cultures.* Roslyn, N.Y.: Ellipsis Arts, 1997. How the other half lives.

Montello, Louise. *Essential Musical Intelligence: Using Music as Your Path to Healing, Creativity, and Radiant Wholeness.* Wheaton, Ill.: Quest Books, 2002. Lots of exercises to aid your development and healing.

Teeguarden, Iona Marsaa. *A Complete Guide to Acupressure: Jin Shin Do.* Tokyo: Japan Publications, 1996.

LITERATURE
The Holy Bible, New Revised Standard Version. Oxford: Oxford University Press, 1998.

Menon, Ramesh. *The Ramayana: A Modern Retelling of the Great Indian Epic.* New York: North Point Press, 2001. Incredible imagery, beautiful prose.

MUSIC

Bonny, Helen L., and Louis M. Savary. *Music and Your Mind: Listening with a New Consciousness.* Barrytown, N.Y.: Station Hill Press, 1973. A classic look at music and imagery.

Campbell, Don. *The Mozart Effect: Tapping the Power of Music to Heal the Body, Strengthen the Mind, and Unlock the Creative Spirit.* New York: Avon Books, 1997.

———. *The Mozart Effect for Children: Awakening Your Child's Mind, Health, and Creativity with Music.* New York: HarperCollins, 2000.

———. *Music: Physician for Times to Come.* Wheaton, Ill.: The Theosophical Publishing House, 1991. This great anthology of music healing and education contains an interview with Alfred Tomatis, in which he tells the story of the monks in chapter 1.

Copland, Aaron. *Music and Imagination.* Cambridge, Mass.: Harvard University Press, 1952.

Davison, Archibald T., and Willi Apel. *Historical Anthology of Music.* Cambridge, Mass.: Harvard University Press, 1946.

Gass, Robert, and Kathleen Brehony. *Chanting: Discovering Spirit in Sound.* New York: Broadway Books, 1999. A multifaith look at chant, with about a dozen tunes.

Hildegard of Bingen. *Lieder.* Salzburg: Otto Müller Verlag, 1969. A complete collection of her chants in notation. Text is in Latin and German.

Jansen, Eva Rudy. *Singing Bowls: A Practical Handbook of Instruction and Use.* Diever, Neth.: Binkey Kok Publications, 1990.

Le Mée, Katharine. *Chant: The Origins, Form, Practice, and Healing Power of Gregorian Chant.* New York: Bell Tower, 1994. Great introduction.

Marks, Kate, comp. *Circle of Song: Songs, Chants, and Dances for Ritual and Celebration.* Amherst, Mass.: Full Circle Press, 1993. The broadest collection of chants.

Parker, Alice. *Melodious Accord: Good Singing in Church.* Chicago: Liturgy Training Publications, 1991.

PRAYER

Ashley-Farrand, Thomas. *Healing Mantras: Using Sound Affirmations for Personal Power, Creativity, and Healing.* New York: Ballantine Wellspring, 1999. Mantras for the planets, healing illnesses and anger, and a Wesak ceremony (Buddha's birthday).

———. *Shakti Mantras: Tapping into the Great Goddess Energy Within.* New York: Ballantine Books, 2003. Filled with chants and stories of goddesses in action.

Barks, Coleman, and John Moyne. *The Drowned Book: Ecstatic and Earthly Reflections of Bahauddin, the Father of Rumi.* San Francisco: HarperSanFrancisco, 2004.

Bittlinger, Arnold. *Archetypal Chakras: Meditations and Exercises for Opening Your Chakras.* York Beach, Maine: Weiser, 2001. A Jungian approach to the chakras, with exercises, including an exercise using the Lord's Prayer.

The Book of Common Prayer. Oxford: Oxford University Press, 1990.

Cantalamessa, Raniero. *Come, Creator Spirit: Meditations on the Veni Creator.* Translated by Denis and Marlene Barrett. Collegeville, Minn.: Liturgical Press, 2003. A book-length meditation on the Veni Creator chant.

Cooper, David A. *A Heart of Stillness: A Complete Guide to Learning the Art of Meditation.* Woodstock, Vt.: SkyLight Paths, 1999. My favorite book on spiritual practice. Monkey mind, pleasant and unpleasant mind states, and how not to get stuck in any of them.

———. *Silence, Simplicity, and Solitude: A Guide to Spiritual Retreat.* Woodstock, Vt.: SkyLight Paths, 1999. The best guide I know for setting up a retreat, either personal or group.

Cunningham, Elizabeth. *Small Bird: Poems and Prayers.* Barrytown, N.Y.: Station Hill Press, 2000.

Falk, Marcia. *The Book of Blessings: New Jewish Prayers for Daily Life, the Sabbath, and the New Moon Festival.* San Francisco:

HarperSanFrancisco, 1996. Stunningly beautiful prayers in English, Hebrew, and transliterated Hebrew.

Hanh, Thich Nhat. *The Miracle of Mindfulness: A Manual of Meditation.* Boston: Beacon Press, 1975.

———. *Peace Is Every Step: The Path of Mindfulness in Everyday Life.* New York: Bantam, 1993. How to cook your potatoes.

Levertov, Denise. *Candles in Babylon.* New York: New Directions, 1978. The Mass for the Day of St. Thomas Didymus is a doubter's delight.

A New Zealand Prayer Book. Auckland: Collins, 1989. "The Lake of Beauty" is here, as well as a modern paraphrase of the Lord's Prayer.

Panikkar, Raimundo, ed. and trans. *The Vedic Experience: Mantramañjarī: An Anthology of the Vedas for Modern Man and Contemporary Celebration.* Berkeley: University of California Press, 1977. This is a massive work, a modern translation of the Vedas for meditation, reading, and public and private devotions.

Prabhavananda, Swami. *The Sermon on the Mount According to Vedanta.* Hollywood, Calif.: Vedanta Press, 1963.

Scherman, Nosson, trans. and annot., Meir Zlotowitz, ed. *The Complete ArtScroll Siddur.* Brooklyn: Mesorah Publications, 1985. This prayer book contains the Bedtime Shema, a ritual for the amelioration of dreams, and lots more.

SPIRITUALITY

Bateson, Gregory. *Steps to an Ecology of Mind: Collected Essays in Anthropology, Psychiatry, Evolution, and Epistemology.* New York: Chandler Publishing Company, 1972.

Bien, Thomas, and Beverly Bien. *Finding the Center Within: The Healing Way of Mindfulness Meditation.* Hoboken, N.J.: John Wiley and Sons, 2003. Practical ways to approach life mindfully.

Blofeld, John. *Bodhisattva of Compassion: The Mystical Tradition of Kuan Yin.* Boston: Shambhala, 1977.

Boucher, Sandy. *Discovering Kwan Yin, Buddhist Goddess of Compassion.* Boston: Beacon Press, 1999. Mostly memoir, but with three Kuan Yin songs and chants.

Boyce-Tillman, June. *The Creative Spirit: Harmonious Living with Hildegard of Bingen.* Harrisburg, Pa.: Morehouse Publishing, 2001. A survey of Hildegard's life and music, focusing on interrelationship.

Fox, Matthew. *Sins of the Spirit, Blessings of the Flesh: Lessons for Transforming Evil in Soul and Society.* New York: Harmony Books, 1999. A look at the seven deadly sins as signs of chakra imbalance.

Heschel, Abraham Joshua. *Man's Quest for God: Studies in Prayer and Symbolism.* New York: Scribner, 1954. Just glorious. I read it every year.

———. *Moral Grandeur and Spiritual Audacity: Essays.* Edited by Susannah Heschel. New York: Farrar, Straus and Giroux, 1996. A great anthology of his writings, topically arranged.

Khalsa, Gurucharan Singh, and Yogi Bhajan. *Breathwalk: Breathing Your Way to a Revitalized Body, Mind, and Spirit.* New York: Broadway Books, 2000. Breathwork extraordinaire. Lots of exercises.

Khan, Hazrat Inayat. *The Mysticism of Sound and Music.* Boston: Shambhala, 1991. He found "a melody in every thought, and a harmony in every feeling," and so will you. Transformative.

Kongtrul, Jamgon. *The Great Path of Awakening: An Easily Accessible Introduction for Ordinary People.* Boston: Shambhala, 1987. A commentary on the Mahayana teaching of the seven points of mind training.

Kornfield, Jack. *The Art of Forgiveness, Lovingkindness, and Peace.* New York: Bantam Books, 2002.

Kushner, Lawrence. *The Book of Letters: A Mystical Hebrew Alphabet.* Woodstock, Vt.: Jewish Lights Publishing, 1990.

———. *God Was in This Place and I, i Did Not Know: Finding Self, Spirituality, and Ultimate Meaning.* Woodstock, Vt.: Jewish Lights Publishing, 1991.

Macy, Joanna, and Molly Young Brown. *Coming Back to Life: Practices to Reconnect Our Lives, Our World*. Stony Creek, Conn.: New Society Publishers, 1998. The group exercises for overcoming despair are worth the price of the book.

Palmer, Parker J. *Let Your Life Speak: Listening for the Voice of Vocation*. San Francisco: Jossey-Bass, 2000. This little book is great for anyone wondering about vocation.

Salzberg, Sharon. *Faith: Trusting Your Own Deepest Experience*. New York: Riverhead Books, 2002. Trust it. Don't forget.

Soares-Prabhu, George M. *The Dharma of Jesus*. Edited by Francis X. D'Sa. Maryknoll, N.Y.: Orbis Books, 2003. A collection of his writings. Especially good look at the beatitudes.

Suzuki, Shunryu. *Not Always So: Practicing the True Spirit of Zen*. New York: HarperCollins, 2002. Always good.

Teresa of Ávila. *Interior Castle*. Translated and edited by E. Allison Peers. Garden City, N.Y.: Doubleday, 1961. A classic in Western mysticism. Read it with the chakras in the back of your mind ...

Thondup, Tulku. *Boundless Healing: Meditation Exercises to Enlighten the Mind and Heal the Body*. Boston: Shambhala, 2000. Lots of good exercises.

Tolstoy, Leo. *The Kingdom of God Is Within You: Christianity Not as a Mystic Religion but as a New Theory of Life*. Lincoln: University of Nebraska Press, 1984.

Williams, Rowan. *Teresa of Ávila*. Harrisburg, Pa.: Morehouse Publishing, 1991.

CDs

Anonymous Four. *An English Ladymass: Medieval Chant and Polyphony*. Harmonia Mundi, 1993.

Berezan, Jennifer. *Returning*. Edge of Wonder Records, 2000.

Chants—Mystiques: Hidden Treasures of a Living Tradition. Polygram Records, 1995. With Alberto Mizrahi, one of the best cantors around. He sings the Shema and much more on this great disc.

Cunningham, Ruth. *Ancient Beginnings.* Open Ear Center, 1996.

Das, Krishna. *Breath of the Heart.* Karuna, 2001. Kirtan! I listened to this CD every day for about six months. His best.

El Din, Hamza. *A Wish.* Sounds True, 1999. Mostly instrumental, with one great chant.

Gass, Robert, comp. *Chant: Spirit in Sound.* Spring Hill, 1999. A two-CD anthology of world chant. Disc one is titled "Ecstasy"; disc two, "Stillness."

Hanh, Thich Nhat, and Sister Chan Khong. *Drops of Emptiness.* Sounds True, 1998. Buddhist chants.

HARC. *HARC: Inside Chants.* HARC, 2004. Some of the chants I live with and wrote about in this book.

Keyrouz, Marie. *Byzantine Chant: Passion and Resurrection.* Harmonia Mundi, 2001.

———. *Sacred Chants of the Orient: Melchite Chants.* Harmonia Mundi, 2001.

———. *Traditional Maronite Chant.* Harmonia Mundi, 1992.

Monks of Senegal. *Keur Moussa.* Sounds True, 1997. This is what happens when Gregorian chant meets Africa. Nine monks from St. Peter's Abbey in Solesmes went to Senegal in 1963 to open a branch office. Beautiful and fun!

Pérès, Marcel/Ensemble Organum. *Corsican Chants from Franciscan Manuscripts.* Harmonia Mundi, 1994. Great ensemble chants; really powerful singing.

Planet Yoga: Music for Yoga, Meditation, and Peace. Karuna, 2002. A two-CD anthology. Disc one contains devotional chants (kirtan); disc two contains music for meditation.

Prayer for Peace. Silver Wave, 2000. Many Native American artists can be found on this one, including Joanne Shenandoah. Sales benefit the World Peace Prayer Society. May peace prevail on earth.

San Antonio Vocal Arts Ensemble. *Ancient Echoes: Music from the Time of Jesus and Jerusalem's Second Temple.* World Library Publications, 2002.

Sequentia: Ensemble for Medieval Music. *Ordo Virtutum: Hildegard von Bingen.* Etcetera Record Company, 1998.

Les tres riches heures du Moyen Age: A Medieval Journey. Harmonia Mundi, 1995. This is a six-CD set, culled from the Harmonia Mundi archives, which is a course in medieval music. The first five discs are all chant, all the time. Stunningly good.

Velez, Glen. *Rhythms of the Chakras.* Gemini Sun, 1998. A rhythm for each of your chakras. Some singing, but mostly in drummer language (ta ka ta ka dum, etc....).

WEB SITES AND AUDIO FILES

For audio files of all the chants and mantras in the book, go to www.anahermusic.com

Abbey of Solesmes. This site has lots of Gregorian chant information. www.solesmes.com

Abwoon Study Circle. Neil Douglas-Klotz and native Middle Eastern mysticism. *Abwoon* is an Aramaic word for the power of the universe to give birth to new life, every instant. Check out the links. www.abwoon.com

C-DEEP (The Center for Devotional Energy & Ecstatic Practice). Founded by Rabbi Shefa Gold and Rachmiel O'Regan, M.A. www.rabbishefagold.com

Dharma Haven. Learn about Tibetan Dharma and medicine. Great teaching stories. www.dharma-haven.org

GIA Publications. Find Taizé recordings here. Just type *Taizé* into the search box and away you go. www.giamusic.com

Gregorian Schola. Here are some great links for finding organizations, recordings, square note neums, and sounds. comp.uark.edu/~rlee/otherchant.html

International Lambdoma Research Institute. If you want to know the

exact frequencies that will vibrate your chakras and your organs, this is the site for you.
members.aol.com/Lambdom3/Chakras.html

Japa Yoga by Sri Swami Sivananda. Here are more rules for saying mantra than you want to know. Keep the faith!
www.sivanandadlshq.org/teachings/japayoga.htm

Morning Practices by Rabbi Goldie Milgram.
www.rebgoldie.com/Morning.htm

Morning Service for Shabbat by Rabbi Goldie Milgram.
www.reclaimingjudaism.org/bmitzvah/morningprint.htm

Om A Hung. Khenchen Gyaltshen Rinpoche teaching the purification ritual.
www.dharma-media.org/media/kagyu/drigung/gyaltshen/omahhung_2000/gyaltshen_omahhung_mfs.html

Om Mani Padme Hum. Essay by His Holiness the Dalai Lama.
www.tibet.com/Buddhism/om-mantra.html

Sanskrit Mantras and Spiritual Power. Thomas Ashley-Farrand's Web site. Listen to the Rama Taraka mantra (Gandhi's mantra), and learn all about mantra at this great site.
www.sanskritmantra.com

Tomatis Method. Look here for help with ADHD, Autism, Dyslexia, Asperger's Syndrome, Down's Syndrome, and more.
www.tomatis.com

Unified Buddhist Church. Thich Nhat Hanh and the community at Plum Village.
www.plumvillage.org

World Prayers. A nice collection of adorations, celebrations, invocations, meditations, and peace prayers.
www.worldprayers.org

Tip: If you type the name of any word or mantra into the Google.com search engine, you will find more information than you can possibly use, and much of it will be great.

INDEX OF CHANTS

ACKNOWLEDGMENTS

I would like to acknowledge all the people who have come before me and created beautiful things for my benefit and for the benefit of all of us, but of course I don't know most of them. Many are long dead, and I take comfort in the fact that I am breathing the same air. Many are secret hearts, people who've been praying for me since forever, that I may not even know: I know you're out there. I'd like to thank God every day in all manifestations, small and great, quirky and poignant; it may look like I forget sometimes, but I know you're in there.

Some people I would like to thank specifically are Joan Lange, my ninth grade English teacher, for opening her heart, teaching me the beauty of poetry, and furnishing experiences that helped to connect words with actions. Thanks also to Don Haines Guidotti for introducing me to Monteverdi, and for giving me a recording of Aaron Copland conducting his own music just because it made me cry when I heard it. Thanks also to the people in all the choirs I've ever sung in, for teaching me more about life and love (and Led Zeppelin) than you can imagine. I extend my undying gratitude to Constancio, who knows the importance of creativity, beauty, and kindness, and who patiently reminds me about the importance of being patient. Thanks to Ruth for long talks, new chants every twenty minutes, for loving the land of intuition, and being willing to travel there with me. I am totally grateful to Julia Huttar Bailey for the one decent photo of me; to Elizabeth Cunningham, for permission to reprint "Heart Prayer"; to the Mother Thunder Mission for the Lord's Prayer; and to Martha, Elizabeth, and Carol for reading along the way. For unadulterated graciousness and her willingness to share, I would like to thank Rabbi Shefa Gold; Pat Cook, for the Gayatri mantra, and for helping me to see every day as a crossroad at which the light is mostly green; and Don Campbell, for teaching me the power of music in healing and education, but most especially for the paper plate dance.

To Jon, for thinking to ask, and to all the folks at Skylight Paths (Sarah, Shelly, Diana, and Mark) for superbly doing all the things people do to make really good books: pretty covers, nice layouts, pages in the right order, no typos, nice catalogs, etc.... and especially to Maura Shaw, who helped me to articulate, clarify, and distill all the things that make sense in this book, and who talked me down from the occasional tree with the gifts of her great talent and skillfulness. I suspect she knows more about what I do than *I* do, but she won't admit it (I tried). As for all the things that don't make sense, and any errors of fact, the fault is surely mine, all mine.

Most importantly, I thank Susan, my sweet, funny, tender love, without whom this book would not be in your hands, and without whom life wouldn't be nearly as breathtaking, wonderful, and secretly surprising.

notes

notes

About SKYLIGHT PATHS Publishing

SkyLight Paths Publishing is creating a place where people of different spiritual traditions come together for challenge and inspiration, a place where we can help each other understand the mystery that lies at the heart of our existence.

Through spirituality, our religious beliefs are increasingly becoming a part of our lives—rather than *apart* from our lives. While many of us may be more interested than ever in spiritual growth, we may be less firmly planted in traditional religion. Yet, we do want to deepen our relationship to the sacred, to learn from our own as well as from other faith traditions, and to practice in new ways.

SkyLight Paths sees both believers and seekers as a community that increasingly transcends traditional boundaries of religion and denomination—people wanting to learn from each other, *walking together, finding the way.*

We at SkyLight Paths take great care to produce beautiful books that present meaningful spiritual content in a form that reflects the art of making high quality books. Therefore, we want to acknowledge those who contributed to the production of this book.

PRODUCTION
Tim Holtz

EDITORIAL
Sarah McBride, Maura D. Shaw & Emily Wichland

COVER DESIGN & ILLUSTRATION
Sara Dismukes

TEXT DESIGN
Susan Ramundo, SR Desktop Services,
Ridge, New York

PRINTING & BINDING
Versa Press, East Peoria, Illinois

Spiritual Biography

The Life of Evelyn Underhill
An Intimate Portrait of the Groundbreaking Author of Mysticism
by *Margaret Cropper;* Foreword by *Dana Greene*

Evelyn Underhill was a passionate writer and teacher who wrote elegantly on mysticism, worship, and devotional life. This is the story of how she made her way toward spiritual maturity, from her early days of agnosticism to the years when her influence was felt throughout the world. 6 x 9, 288 pp, 5 b/w photos, Quality PB, ISBN 1-893361-70-5 **$18.95**

Zen Effects: *The Life of Alan Watts*
by *Monica Furlong*

The first and only full-length biography of one of the most charismatic spiritual leaders of the twentieth century—now back in print!

Through his widely popular books and lectures, Alan Watts (1915–1973) did more to introduce Eastern philosophy and religion to Western minds than any figure before or since. Here is the only biography of this charismatic figure, who served as Zen teacher, Anglican priest, lecturer, academic, entertainer, a leader of the San Francisco renaissance, and author of more than 30 books, including *The Way of Zen, Psychotherapy East and West* and *The Spirit of Zen.* 6 x 9, 264 pp, Quality PB, ISBN 1-893361-32-2 **$16.95**

   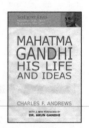

Simone Weil: *A Modern Pilgrimage*
by *Robert Coles*

The extraordinary life of the spiritual philosopher who's been called both saint and madwoman.

The French writer and philosopher Simone Weil (1906–1943) devoted her life to a search for God—while avoiding membership in organized religion. Robert Coles' intriguing study of Weil details her short, eventful life, and is an insightful portrait of the beloved and controversial thinker whose life and writings influenced many (from T. S. Eliot to Adrienne Rich to Albert Camus), and continue to inspire seekers everywhere. 6 x 9, 208 pp, Quality PB, ISBN 1-893361-34-9 **$16.95**

Mahatma Gandhi: *His Life and Ideas*
by *Charles F. Andrews;* Foreword by *Dr. Arun Gandhi*

An intimate biography of one of the greatest social and religious reformers of the modern world.

Examines from a contemporary Christian activist's point of view the religious ideas and political dynamics that influenced the birth of the peaceful resistance movement, the primary tool that Gandhi and the people of his homeland would use to gain India its freedom from British rule. An ideal introduction to the life and life's work of this great spiritual leader. 6 x 9, 336 pp, 5 b/w photos, Quality PB, ISBN 1-893361-89-6 **$18.95**

Meditation/Prayer

Finding Grace at the Center: *The Beginning of Centering Prayer*
by *M. Basil Pennington, OCSO, Thomas Keating, OCSO,* and *Thomas E. Clarke, SJ*

The book that helped launch the Centering Prayer "movement." Explains the prayer of *The Cloud of Unknowing,* posture and relaxation, the three simple rules of centering prayer, and how to cultivate centering prayer throughout all aspects of your life.

5 x 7¼,112 pp, HC, ISBN 1-893361-69-1 **$14.95**

Prayers to an Evolutionary God
by *William Cleary;* Afterword by *Diarmuid O'Murchu*

How is it possible to pray when God is dislocated from heaven, dispersed all around us, and more of a creative force than an all-knowing father? In this unique collection of eighty prose prayers and related commentary, William Cleary considers new ways of thinking about God and the world around us. Inspired by the spiritual and scientific teachings of Diarmuid O'Murchu and Teilhard de Chardin, Cleary reveals that religion and science can be combined to create an expanding view of the universe—an evolutionary faith.

6 x 9, 208 pp, HC, ISBN 1-59473-006-7 **$21.99**

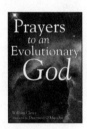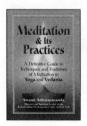

Meditation without Gurus
A Guide to the Heart of Practice
by *Clark Strand*

Short, compelling reflections show you how to make meditation a part of your daily life, without the complication of gurus, mantras, retreats, or treks to distant mountains. This enlightening book strips the practice down to its essential heart—simplicity, lightness, and peace—showing you that the most important part of practice is not whether you can get in the full lotus position, but rather your ability to become fully present in the moment.

5½ x 8½, 192 pp, Quality PB, ISBN 1-893361-93-4 **$16.95**

Meditation & Its Practices
A Definitive Guide to Techniques and Traditions of Meditation in Yoga and Vedanta
by *Swami Adiswarananda*

The complete sourcebook for exploring Hinduism's two most time-honored traditions of meditation.

Drawing on both classic and contemporary sources, this comprehensive sourcebook outlines the scientific, psychological, and spiritual elements of Yoga and Vedanta meditation.

6 x 9, 504 pp, HC, ISBN 1-893361-83-7 **$34.95**

Spiritual Practice

The Sacred Art of Bowing
Preparing to Practice
by *Andi Young*

This informative and inspiring introduction to bowing—and related spiritual practices—shows you how to do it, why it's done, and what spiritual benefits it has to offer. Incorporates interviews, personal stories, illustrations of bowing in practice, advice on how you can incorporate bowing into your daily life, and how bowing can deepen spiritual understanding.
5½ x 8½, 128 pp, b/w illus., Quality PB, ISBN 1-893361-82-9 **$14.95**

Praying with Our Hands: *Twenty-One Practices of Embodied Prayer from the World's Spiritual Traditions*
by *Jon M. Sweeney;* Photographs by *Jennifer J. Wilson;*
Foreword by *Mother Tessa Bielecki;* Afterword by *Taitetsu Unno, PhD*

A spiritual guidebook for bringing prayer into our bodies.

This inspiring book of reflections and accompanying photographs shows us twenty-one simple ways of using our hands to speak to God, to enrich our devotion and ritual. All express the various approaches of the world's religious traditions to bringing the body into worship. Spiritual traditions represented include Anglican, Sufi, Zen, Roman Catholic, Yoga, Shaker, Hindu, Jewish, Pentecostal, Eastern Orthodox, and many others.
8 x 8, 96 pp, 22 duotone photographs, Quality PB, ISBN 1-893361-16-0 **$16.95**

   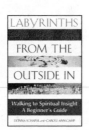

The Sacred Art of Listening
Forty Reflections for Cultivating a Spiritual Practice
by *Kay Lindahl;* Illustrations by *Amy Schnapper*

More than ever before, we need to embrace the skills and practice of listening. You will learn to: Speak clearly from your heart • Communicate with courage and compassion • Heighten your awareness for deep listening • Enhance your ability to listen to people with different belief systems. 8 x 8, 160 pp, Illus., Quality PB, ISBN 1-893361-44-6 **$16.99**

Labyrinths from the Outside In
Walking to Spiritual Insight—A Beginner's Guide
by *Donna Schaper* and *Carole Ann Camp*

The user-friendly, interfaith guide to making and using labyrinths— for meditation, prayer, and celebration.

Labyrinth walking is a spiritual exercise *anyone* can do. This accessible guide unlocks the mysteries of the labyrinth for all of us, providing ideas for using the labyrinth walk for prayer, meditation, and celebrations to mark the most important moments in life. Includes instructions for making a labyrinth of your own and finding one in your area.
6 x 9, 208 pp, b/w illus. and photographs, Quality PB, ISBN 1-893361-18-7 **$16.95**

SkyLight Illuminations Series
Andrew Harvey, series editor

Offers today's spiritual seeker an enjoyable entry into the great classic texts of the world's spiritual traditions. Each classic is presented in an accessible translation, with facing pages of guided commentary from experts, giving you the keys you need to understand the history, context, and meaning of the text. This series enables readers of all backgrounds to experience and understand classic spiritual texts directly, and to make them a part of their lives. Andrew Harvey writes the foreword to each volume, an insightful, personal introduction to each classic.

Bhagavad Gita: *Annotated & Explained*
Translation by *Shri Purohit Swami;* Annotation by *Kendra Crossen Burroughs*

"The very best Gita for first-time readers." —Ken Wilber

Millions of people turn daily to India's most beloved holy book, whose universal appeal has made it popular with non-Hindus and Hindus alike. This edition introduces you to the characters, explains references and philosophical terms, shares the interpretations of famous spiritual leaders and scholars, and more. 5½ x 8½, 192 pp, Quality PB, ISBN 1-893361-28-4 **$16.95**

  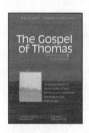 

The Way of a Pilgrim: *Annotated & Explained*
Translation and annotation by *Gleb Pokrovsky*

This classic of Russian spirituality is the delightful account of one man who sets out to learn the prayer of the heart—also known as the "Jesus prayer"—and how the practice transforms his life. 5½ x 8½, 160 pp, Illus., Quality PB, ISBN 1-893361-31-4 **$14.95**

The Gospel of Thomas: *Annotated & Explained*
Translation and annotation by *Stevan Davies*

Discovered in 1945, this collection of aphoristic sayings sheds new light on the origins of Christianity and the intriguing figure of Jesus, portraying the Kingdom of God as a present fact about the world, rather than a future promise or future threat. This edition guides you through the text with annotations that focus on the meaning of the sayings. 5½ x 8½, 192 pp, Quality PB, ISBN 1-893361-45-4 **$16.95**

Rumi and Islam: *Selections from His Stories, Poems, and Discourses—Annotated & Explained*
Translation and annotation by *Ibrahim Gamard*

Offers a new way of thinking about Rumi's poetry. Ibrahim Gamard focuses on Rumi's place within the Sufi tradition of Islam, providing you with insight into the mystical side of the religion—one that has love of God at its core and sublime wisdom teachings as its pathways. 5½ x 8½, 240 pp, Quality PB, ISBN 1-59473-002-4 **$15.99**

SkyLight Illuminations Series
Andrew Harvey, series editor

Zohar: *Annotated & Explained*
Translation and annotation by *Daniel C. Matt*

The cornerstone text of Kabbalah.

The best-selling author of *The Essential Kabbalah* brings together in one place the most important teachings of the *Zohar*, the canonical text of Jewish mystical tradition. Guides you step by step through the midrash, mystical fantasy, and Hebrew scripture that make up the *Zohar*, explaining the inner meanings in facing-page commentary. Ideal for readers without any prior knowledge of Jewish mysticism.
5½ x 8½, 176 pp, Quality PB, ISBN 1-893361-51-9 **$15.99**

Selections from the Gospel of Sri Ramakrishna
Annotated & Explained
Translation by *Swami Nikhilananda;* Annotation by *Kendra Crossen Burroughs*

The words of India's greatest example of God-consciousness and mystical ecstasy in recent history.

Introduces the fascinating world of the Indian mystic and the universal appeal of his message that has inspired millions of devotees for more than a century. Selections from the original text and insightful yet unobtrusive commentary highlight the most important and inspirational teachings. Ideal for readers without any prior knowledge of Hinduism.
5½ x 8½, 240 pp, b/w photographs, Quality PB, ISBN 1-893361-46-2 **$16.95**

Dhammapada: *Annotated & Explained*
Translation by *Max Müller* and revised by *Jack Maguire;* Annotation by *Jack Maguire*

The classic of Buddhist spiritual practice.

The Dhammapada—words spoken by the Buddha himself over 2,500 years ago—is notoriously difficult to understand for the first-time reader. Now you can experience it with understanding even if you have no previous knowledge of Buddhism. Enlightening facing-page commentary explains all the names, terms, and references, giving you deeper insight into the text.
5½ x 8½, 160 pp, b/w photographs, Quality PB, ISBN 1-893361-42-X **$14.95**

Hasidic Tales: *Annotated & Explained*
Translation and annotation by *Rabbi Rami Shapiro*

The legendary tales of the impassioned Hasidic rabbis.

The allegorical quality of Hasidic tales can be perplexing. Here, they are presented as stories rather than parables, making them accessible and meaningful. Each demonstrates the spiritual power of unabashed joy, offers lessons for leading a holy life, and reminds us that the Divine can be found in the everyday. Annotations explain theological concepts, introduce major characters, and clarify references unfamiliar to most readers.
5½ x 8½, 240 pp, Quality PB, ISBN 1-893361-86-1 **$16.95**

Children's Spirituality

Because Nothing Looks Like God
by *Lawrence and Karen Kushner*
Full-color illus. by
Dawn W. Majewski

For ages
4 & up

MULTICULTURAL, NONDENOMINATIONAL,
NONSECTARIAN

Real-life examples of happiness and sadness—from
goodnight stories, to the hope and fear felt the first
time at bat, to the closing moments of life—introduce
children to the possibilities of spiritual life. A vibrant way for children—and their adults—
to explore what, where, and how God is in our lives.

11 x 8½, 32 pp, HC, Full-color illus., ISBN 1-58023-092-X **$16.95**
*Also available: **Teacher's Guide**, 8½ x 11, 22 pp, PB, ISBN 1-58023-140-3* **$6.95** For ages 5–8

Where Is God? (A Board Book)
by *Lawrence and Karen Kushner*; Full-color illus. by *Dawn W. Majewski*

For ages
0–4

A gentle way for young children to explore how God is with us every day, in every way. Abridged
from *Because Nothing Looks Like God* by Lawrence and Karen Kushner and specially adapted
to board book format to delight and inspire young readers.
5 x 5, 24 pp, Board, Full-color illus., ISBN 1-893361-17-9 **$7.95**

What Does God Look Like? (A Board Book)
by *Lawrence and Karen Kushner*; Full-color illus. by *Dawn W. Majewski*

For ages
0–4

A simple way for young children to explore the ways that we "see" God. Abridged from *Because
Nothing Looks Like God* by Lawrence and Karen Kushner and specially adapted to board book
format to delight and inspire young readers.
5 x 5, 24 pp, Board, Full-color illus., ISBN 1-893361-23-3 **$7.95**

How Does God Make Things Happen? (A Board Book)
by *Lawrence and Karen Kushner*; Full-color illus. by *Dawn W. Majewski*

For ages
0–4

A charming invitation for young children to explore how God makes things happen in our
world. Abridged from *Because Nothing Looks Like God* by Lawrence and Karen Kushner
and specially adapted to board book format to delight and inspire young readers.
5 x 5, 24 pp, Board, Full-color illus., ISBN 1-893361-24-1 **$7.95**

What Is God's Name? (A Board Book)
by *Sandy Eisenberg Sasso*; Full-color illus. by *Phoebe Stone*

For ages
0–4

Everyone and everything in the world has a name. What is God's name? Abridged from the
award-winning *In God's Name* by Sandy Eisenberg Sasso and specially adapted to board
book format to delight and inspire young readers.
5 x 5, 24 pp, Board, Full-color illus., ISBN 1-893361-10-1 **$7.99**

Children's Spirituality

MULTICULTURAL, NONDENOMINATIONAL, NONSECTARIAN

•Award Winner•

Where Does God Live?
For ages 3–6

by *August Gold* and *Matthew J. Perlman*

Using simple, everyday examples that children can relate to, this colorful book helps young readers develop a personal understanding of God.

10 x 8½, 32 pp, Quality PB, Full-color photo illus.,
ISBN 1-893361-39-X **$8.99**

•Award Winner•

•Award Winner•

•Award Winner•

God in Between
For ages 4 & up

by *Sandy Eisenberg Sasso;* Full-color illus. by *Sally Sweetland*

If you wanted to find God, where would you look? A magical, mythical tale that teaches that God can be found where we are: within all of us and the relationships between us. "This happy and wondrous book takes our children on a sweet and holy journey into God's presence." —Rabbi Wayne Dosick, PhD, author of *The Business Bible* and *Soul Judaism*
9 x 12, 32 pp, HC, Full-color illus., ISBN 1-879045-86-9 **$16.95**

Cain & Abel: *Finding the Fruits of Peace*
For ages 5 & up

by *Sandy Eisenberg Sasso;* Full-color illus. by *Joani Keller Rothenberg*

A sensitive recasting of the ancient tale shows we have the power to deal with anger in positive ways. Provides questions for kids and adults to explore together. "Editor's Choice"—American Library Association's *Booklist* 9 x 12, 32 pp, HC, Full-color illus., ISBN 1-58023-123-3 **$16.95**

In Our Image: *God's First Creatures*
For ages 4 & up

by *Nancy Sohn Swartz;* Full-color illus. by *Melanie Hall*

A playful new twist on the Creation story—from the perspective of the animals. Celebrates the interconnectedness of nature and the harmony of all living things. "The vibrantly colored illustrations nearly leap off the page in this delightful interpretation." —*School Library Journal*
"A message all children should hear, presented in words and pictures that children will find irresistible." —Rabbi Harold Kushner, author of *When Bad Things Happen to Good People*
9 x 12, 32 pp, HC, Full-color illus., ISBN 1-879045-99-0 **$16.95**

Children's Spiritual Biography

Ten Amazing People
And How They Changed the World

For ages 7 & up

by *Maura D. Shaw*; Foreword by *Dr. Robert Coles*
Full-color illus. by *Stephen Marchesi*

Black Elk • Dorothy Day • Malcolm X • Mahatma Gandhi •
Martin Luther King, Jr. • Mother Teresa • Janusz Korczak •
Desmond Tutu • Thich Nhat Hanh • Albert Schweitzer

This vivid, inspirational, and authoritative book will open new possibilities for children by telling the stories of how ten of the past century's greatest leaders changed the world in important ways.

8½ x 11, 48 pp, HC, Full-color illus., ISBN 1-893361-47-0 **$17.95**

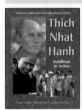
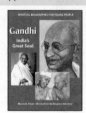

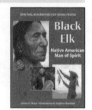

A new series: Spiritual Biographies for Young People

Thich Nhat Hanh: *Buddhism in Action*

For ages 7 & up

by *Maura D. Shaw*; Full-color illus. by *Stephen Marchesi*

Warm illustrations, photos, age-appropriate activities, and Thich Nhat Hanh's own poems introduce a great man to children in a way they can understand and enjoy. Includes a list of important Buddhist words to know.

6¼ x 8¼, 32 pp, HC, Full-color illus., ISBN 1-893361-87-X **$12.95**

Gandhi: *India's Great Soul*

For ages 7 & up

by *Maura D. Shaw*; Full-color illus. by *Stephen Marchesi*

There are a number of biographies of Gandhi written for young readers, but this is the only one that balances a simple text with illustrations, photographs, and activities that encourage children and adults to talk about how to make changes happen without violence. Introduces children to important concepts of freedom, equality, and justice among people of all backgrounds and religions.

6¼ x 8¼, 32 pp, HC, Full-color illus., ISBN 1-893361-91-8 **$12.95**

Dorothy Day: *A Catholic Life of Action*

For ages 7 & up

by *Maura D. Shaw*; Full-color illus. by *Stephen Marchesi*

Introduces children to one of the most inspiring women of the twentieth century, a down-to-earth spiritual leader who saw the presence of God in every person she met. Includes practical activities, a timeline, and a list of important words to know.

6¼ x 8¼, 32 pp, HC, Full-color illus., ISBN 1-59473-011-3 **$12.99**

Black Elk: *Native American Man of Spirit*

For ages 7 & up

by *Maura D. Shaw*; Full-color illus. by *Stephen Marchesi*

Through historically accurate illustrations and photos, inspiring age-appropriate activities, and Black Elk's own words, this colorful biography introduces children to a remarkable person who ensured that the traditions and beliefs of his people would not be forgotten.

6¼ x 8¼, 32 pp, HC, Full-color illus., ISBN 1-59473-043-1 **$12.99**

Global Spiritual Perspectives

Spiritual Perspectives on America's Role as Superpower
by *the Editors at SkyLight Paths*

Are we the world's good neighbor or a global bully?

Explores broader issues surrounding the use of American power around the world, including in Iraq and the Middle East. From a spiritual perspective, what are America's responsibilities as the only remaining superpower?

Contributors:

Dr. Beatrice Bruteau • Rev. Dr. Joan Brown Campbell • Tony Campolo • Rev. Forrest Church • Lama Surya Das • Matthew Fox • Kabir Helminski • Thich Nhat Hanh • Eboo Patel • Abbot M. Basil Pennington, ocso • Dennis Prager • Rosemary Radford Ruether • Wayne Teasdale • Rev. William McD. Tully • Rabbi Arthur Waskow • John Wilson

5½ x 8½, 256 pp, Quality PB, ISBN 1-893361-81-0 **$16.95**

 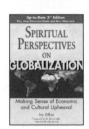 

Spiritual Perspectives on Globalization, 2nd Edition
Making Sense of Economic and Cultural Upheaval
by *Ira Rifkin*; Foreword by *Dr. David Little, Harvard Divinity School*

What is globalization? What are spiritually minded people saying and doing about it?

This lucid introduction surveys the religious landscape, explaining in clear and nonjudgmental language the beliefs that motivate spiritual leaders, activists, theologians, academics, and others involved on all sides of the issue. This edition includes a new Afterword and Discussion Guide designed for group use.

5½ x 8½, 256 pp, Quality PB, ISBN 1-59473-045-8 **$16.99**

Spiritual Innovators: *Seventy-Five Extraordinary People Who Changed the World in the Past Century*
Edited by *Ira Rifkin* and *the Editors at SkyLight Paths*; Foreword by *Robert Coles*

Black Elk, Bede Griffiths, H. H. the Dalai Lama, Abraham Joshua Heschel, Martin Luther King, Jr., Krishnamurti, C. S. Lewis, Aimee Semple McPherson, Thomas Merton, Simone Weil, and many more.

Profiles of the most important spiritual leaders of the past one hundred years. An invaluable reference of twentieth-century religion and an inspiring resource for spiritual challenge today. Authoritative list of seventy-five includes mystics and martyrs, intellectuals and charismatics from the East and West. For each, includes a brief biography, inspiring quotes, and resources for more in-depth study.

6 x 9, 304 pp, b/w photographs, Quality PB, ISBN 1-893361-50-0 **$16.95**; HC, ISBN 1-893361-43-8 **$24.95**

Religious Etiquette/Reference

How to Be a Perfect Stranger, 3rd Edition
The Essential Religious Etiquette Handbook
Edited by *Stuart M. Matlins* and *Arthur J. Magida*

The indispensable guidebook to help the well-meaning guest when visiting other people's religious ceremonies.

A straightforward guide to the rituals and celebrations of the major religions and denominations in the United States and Canada from the perspective of an interested guest of any other faith, based on information obtained from authorities of each religion. Belongs in every living room, library, and office.

COVERS:

African American Methodist Churches • Assemblies of God • Baha'i • Baptist • Buddhist • Christian Church (Disciples of Christ) • Christian Science (Church of Christ, Scientist) • Churches of Christ • Episcopalian and Anglican • Hindu • Islam • Jehovah's Witnesses • Jewish • Lutheran • Mennonite/Amish • Methodist • Mormon (Church of Jesus Christ of Latter-day Saints) • Native American/First Nations • Orthodox Churches • Pentecostal Church of God • Presbyterian • Quaker (Religious Society of Friends) • Reformed Church in America/Canada • Roman Catholic • Seventh-day Adventist • Sikh • Unitarian Universalist • United Church of Canada • United Church of Christ

6 x 9, 432 pp, Quality PB, ISBN 1-893361-67-5 **$19.95**

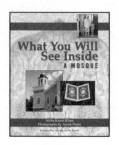

What You Will See Inside a Mosque
by *Aisha Karen Khan*; Photographs by *Aaron Pepis*

A colorful, fun-to-read introduction that explains the ways and whys of Muslim faith and worship.

Visual and informative, featuring full-page pictures and concise descriptions of what is happening, the objects used, the spiritual leaders and laypeople who have specific roles, and the spiritual intent of the believers.

Ideal for children as well as teachers, parents, librarians, clergy, and lay leaders who want to demystify the celebrations and ceremonies of Islam throughout the year, as well as encourage understanding and tolerance among different faith traditions.

8½ x 10½, 32 pp, Full-color photographs, HC, ISBN 1-893361-60-8 **$16.95**

Interspirituality

A Walk with Four Spiritual Guides
Krishna, Buddha, Jesus, and Ramakrishna
by *Andrew Harvey*

Andrew Harvey's warm and personal introduction to each guide offers his own experiences of learning from their wisdom.

Krishna, Buddha, Jesus, Ramakrishna: four of the world's most interesting and challenging spiritual masters. The core of their most important teachings—along with annotations from expert scholars and introductions from Andrew Harvey, one of the great spiritual thinkers of our time—now are all in one beautiful volume.

5½ x 8½, 192 pp, 10 b/w photos & illus., Hardcover, ISBN 1-893361-73-X **$21.95**

The Alphabet of Paradise: *An A–Z of Spirituality for Everyday Life*
by *Howard Cooper*

"An extraordinary book." —Karen Armstrong

One of the most eloquent new voices in spirituality, Howard Cooper takes us on a journey of discovery—into ourselves and into the past—to find the signposts that can help us live more meaningful lives. In twenty-six engaging chapters—from A to Z—Cooper spiritually illuminates the subjects of daily life, using an ancient Jewish mystical method of interpretation that reveals both the literal and more allusive meanings of each. Topics include: Awe, Bodies, Creativity, Dreams, Emotions, Sports, and more.

5 x 7¼, 224 pp, Quality PB, ISBN 1-893361-80-2 **$16.95**

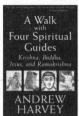   

Daughters of the Desert: *Tales of Remarkable Women from Christian, Jewish, and Muslim Traditions*
by *Claire Rudolf Murphy, Meghan Nuttall Sayres, Mary Cronk Farrell, Sarah Conover,* and *Betsy Wharton*

Breathes new life into the old tales of our female ancestors in faith.

The authors use traditional scriptural passages as their starting points, then with vivid detail fill in historical context and place. Chapters reveal the voices of Sarah, Hagar, Huldah, Esther, Salome, Mary Magdalene, Lydia, Khadija, Fatima, and many more. Historical fiction ideal for readers of all ages. 5½ x 8½, 192 pp, HC, ISBN 1-893361-72-1 **$19.95**

Bede Griffiths: *An Introduction to His Interspiritual Thought*
by *Wayne Teasdale*

The first in-depth study of Bede Griffiths' contemplative experience and thought.

Wayne Teasdale, a longtime personal friend and student of Griffiths, creates in this intimate portrait an intriguing view into the beliefs and life of this champion of interreligious acceptance and harmony. Explains key terms that form the basis of Griffiths' contemplative understanding, and the essential characteristics of his theology as they relate to the Hindu and Christian traditions.

6 x 9, 288 pp, Quality PB, ISBN 1-893361-77-2 **$18.95**

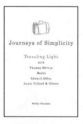
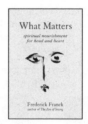
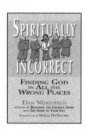